Contents

To my brother Robin Clarke

The Time of the Communities

Therapeutic Communities

Series editors: Rex Haigh and Jan Lees

The Therapeutic Community movement holds a multidisciplinary view of health which is based on ideas of collective responsibility, citizenship and empowerment. The tradition has a long and distinguished history and is experiencing a revival of interest in contemporary theory and practice. It draws from many different principles – including analytic, behavioural, creative, educational and humanistic – in the framework of a group-based view of the social origins and maintenance of much overwhelming distress, mental ill-health and deviant behaviour. Therapeutic Community principles are applicable in a wide variety of settings, and this series reflects that.

Therapeutic Communities for Children and Young People
Therapeutic Communities 10
Edited by Adrian Ward, Kajetan Kasinski, Jane Pooley, Alan Worthington
ISBN 1 84310 096 7

Thinking About Institutions
Milieux and Madness
Therapeutic Communities 8
R.D. Hinshelwood
ISBN 1 85302 954 8

A Therapeutic Community Approach to Care in the Community
Dialogue and Dwelling
Edited by Sarah Tucker
Therapeutic Communities 3
ISBN 1 85302 751 0

Therapeutic Communities
Past, Present and Future
Therapeutic Communities 2
Edited by Penelope Campling and Rex Haigh
ISBN 1 85302 626 3

Introduction to Therapeutic Communities
Therapeutic Communities 1
David Kennard
ISBN 1 85302 603 4

The Time of the Communities

People, Places, Events

Liam Clarke

Therapeutic Communities 12

Jessica Kingsley Publishers
London and New York

First published in the United Kingdom in 2004
by Jessica Kingsley Publishers Ltd
116 Pentonville Road
London N1 9JB, England
and
29 West 35th Street, 10th fl.
New York, NY 10001-2299, USA

www.jkp.com

Copyright © Liam Clarke 2004

Library of Congress Cataloging in Publication Data
A CIP catalog record for this book is available from the Library of Congress

British Library Cataloguing in Publication Data
A CIP catalogue record for this book is available from the British Library

ISBN 1 84310 128 9

Printed and Bound in Great Britain by
Athenaeum Press, Gateshead, Tyne and Wear

Historical Preface

> History in any of these cases is its own measure of significance and touchstone of worth.

> Raphael Samuel (1994)

It is doubtful whether 'grand periods' such as the Enlightenment or the Renaissance ever existed, or that we can justify using the Seventies and 'glam rock', the Fifties and 'you've never had it so good' or the Sixties and 'the invention of sex' so as to make comparisons and contrasts between them. According to Arthur Marwick, 'We readily think in decades but that is only because we count the years as we would our fingers or our toes' (Marwick 1998, p.5). Naturally, historians have 'an analytical need' to do this, some more than others. One occasionally sees a history of Europe or of the world but usually chopped into digestible pieces in order to make the reader's journey easier.

History, of course, is not the past: it is versions of the past. No wonder Henry Ford could say that 'History is Bunk'. You really only need it if you choose to need it. Some make heavy weather of it; Winston Churchill said that without the past, the future becomes less certain. He meant, of course, *his* version of the past, which he frequently called upon so as to further the aims of the present.

The classic formulation of this tendency was what Herbert Butterfield called the Whig Interpretation of History, where 'the study of the past with the past with one eye, so to speak, upon the present [becomes] the source of all sins and sophistries in history' (Butterfield 1931, p.11).

Participants' views

Not to do this is very difficult; it requires self control as well as a willingness to subject one's interests to the rigours of technique and method. One 'technique' which may help is to take account of participants' views wherever possible: the basic premise here is that understanding 'what happened' means looking at the experiences of as many of those involved as possible.

In his history of Earlswood Asylum, Wright (2001) constructs his narrative 'from below', a phrase he attributes to the late Roy Porter (1985). His approach is to show how people – in this case patients, doctors, nurses – have experienced the asylum world and how they articulate its relevance to their lives. The stress is on interaction: meaning lies with the various players as they move around and within the context of their hospital.

Although there are examples from the early part of the last century, it was only in the 1960s that histories of health and illness, based on the narratives of those involved, took shape. Till then, a Whig style of linear development – dotted here and there by the achievements of Great Medical Men – held sway. In psychiatry, the manner of contradicting this has been to produce social histories of particular institutions and the light they throw on asylum care in general. In addition to Wright's study, for example, there is Digby's account of the York Retreat (1985) and Malcolm's (1989) history of St Patrick's, Dublin.

Psychiatry, however, has also borne the brunt of revisionist historians eager to recast it as something about which we should be suspicious and vigilant. Major texts by Andrew Scull (1979) and Michel Foucault (1971) have imbued psychiatric practice with malevolent intent. Foucault argues that the Victorian mental hospitals served the function of housing people of little value to burgeoning capitalist systems, whilst Scull sees madness as something that was manufactured to advance the vested interests of medical practitioners. These revisionists, in turn, have had doubts cast on *their* intentions: they have been accused of twisting 'the facts' in support of their ideological views. Shorter (1997, p.331) calls them 'zealot-scholars' saying that they use history to further their anti-psychiatric beliefs. Shorter, cognisant of the pitfalls of his critique, deflects similar criticisms being levelled against *him* with the disarming admission that he is a 'neoapologist' (p.viii). This serves the function of not claiming total impartiality whilst distancing himself from those (apologists) who write 'grand and glorious' stories of medical achievement. However, Dr Shorter then proceeds to do exactly what his 'objective' brand of psychiatry stands accused of by revisionists such as Scull and Foucault:

> Although the skills of the psychologist and social worker are not to be denigrated, the history of medicine suggests that patients derive some kind of bonus from the knowledge that they are dealing with a physician. It seems to be true that the kind of catharsis achieved from telling one's story to a figure of respect is heightened when that figure is not merely a friend or confidante but a doctor. (Shorter 1997, p.327)

Nurses

The case of nurses nicely indicates the problem of perspective in so far as nurses are woven into the web and weave of mental health history but always as a silent majority. Typically, they have provided little information about events of which they have been part. In addition, and for whatever reasons, professional historians have neglected nurses, especially psychiatric nurses, with some histories of nursing barely mentioning psychiatry at all. What these histories represent is, 'a substantial gap between the Whig accounts of progress and enlightenment and the mundane reality of life on the average ward in the average mental and mental deficiency hospital' (Dingwall *et al.* 1988, p.135).

Today, an emergent qualitative literature more accurately reflects things 'on the ground', even if sometimes at odds with the received wisdom of official sources. Nolan's interviews show that, following the 1930 Mental Health Act, whilst:

> psychiatry was generating a compassionate and scientific rhetoric, the rhetoric was limited by those who were expected to implement it. The vast majority of nursing staff were poorly educated working-class people who happily settled for institutionalised life which relieved them of taking decisions or of thinking for themselves. (Nolan 1986, p.21)

Whatever the 'theoretical progression' then holding sway, it did not mirror the underlying views of practitioners which, whatever these might have been, were weighted down by the unrelenting task of getting through the work load. Pagels (1982, p.530) notes how events are often represented as the literary productions of a minority and that these ignore the preoccupations of the many. As we shall see, the prognostications of a handful of medical superintendents, in respect of unlocking mental hospital doors in the 1950s, hardly echoed undercurrents of disaffection from the nurses. More information needs to be obtained from nurses about these events. The problem is that, in treatment settings, nurses are often 'reduced' to being intermediaries between doctors, patients and other professionals to the point that even communicating amongst themselves becomes restricted.

Practice

Arthur Marwick (1982) identifies Peter Winch's *The Idea of a Social Science and its Relation to Philosophy* (1958) as making the important point that analyses, if they are to be worthwhile, should be philosophical in character and connect with questions about the nature of things; they should not get hung up on language. As A. H. Halsey says, 'The point of sociology, after all, is to do it not to talk about it' (Halsey 1995, p.viii).

And the point of therapeutic communities – the subject of this book – is exactly the same. For if anything characterised what therapeutic communities were about it was *doing*, constructing milieus where people could re-examine and, to some extent, reconstruct their lives. That this can proceed without conceptual scepticism is hardly likely: nevertheless, psychiatry is a practice-based activity and therapeutic communities ought to be living, talking, breathing entities. Writing of their history, therefore, has to recognise that there are few facts and many perspectives. Until now, history credited some of these more than others and this has been important in how the relevance of therapeutic communities is currently perceived. One study in particular, published in 1960 by Robert Rapoport, has acquired a dominant, everlasting, role in determining how therapeutic communities are defined.

Considering the facts

Considering whether 'ultimate' or definitive history can be established – the facts once and for all – Sir George Clarke took the view that such a prospect was elusive: historians, he said:

> expect their work to be superseded again and again. They consider that knowledge of the past has come down through one or more human minds, has been processed by them, and therefore cannot consist of elemental and impersonal atoms which nothing can alter…the exploration seems to be endless. (in Carr 1990, pp.7–8)

The listing of historical 'facts' is underscored in Britain by an empiricist tradition which treats a fact as something that can not in itself affect (or be affected by) consciousness: good history – and good research – deals with facts and what falls outside of that is unscientific. Hence the tendency in some quarters to treat qualitative studies as not 'proper' research at all. Or, the belief by others that conditions such as schizophrenia are objective entities and not subjective experiences which need to be listened to and understood. The British tradition is sceptical of interpretation (and intellectualising), preferring, on balance, deductions based on empirically established facts. This, though, tells us little about what to do with facts once we have assembled them. It would be a boring history that listed items whilst shirking their interpretation and, in any event, what we count as fact is largely due to successive historians validating each other's work and in the process giving rise to 'facts'.

In other words, that something did 'in fact' happen is substantiated by scholastic agreements about what significance to attach to this or that event. Significant to whom, of course, is the key question: an account of Henry VIII's Court by a courtier tells us how the Court may have worked from the inside but little about how outsiders saw or were affected by it.

When in 1960, at the invitation of Maxwell Jones, the anthropologist Robert Rapoport and his team went to The Henderson Hospital, their conclusions led to a formulation of therapeutic community practice (communalism, reality confrontation, permissiveness and democratisation) that was subsequently accepted by many as a given. Little credence was attached to these four principles as *interpretations* by a particular group of observers. In addition, that not all of the subjects in the study displayed evidence of working to these principles – quite the contrary in some cases – has been played down.

We shall see (in Chapter 7), in respect of another community, how a single account also dominated people's perceptions of it albeit, on this occasion, with little other information to go on. This unit, called Villa 21, began in 1962 and its founder, David Cooper (1970), has provided a 'warts and all', but essentially positive, account of its progress. However, his story, whilst running parallel to, is curiously at odds with, Clancy Sigal's (1976) account, written as a novel, and anything but positive.

These writers want us to believe certain things: writers seek to persuade us and history comes to us through them. The reason we know precious little about psychiatric nurses is because they were reluctant to write anything down and we shall come across this time and again. Their views are articulated via the representations of others, the classical paradigm of history. So:

> Study the historian before you begin to study the facts. This is, after all, not very abstruse. It is what is already done by the intelligent undergraduate who, when recommended to read a work by the great scholar Jones Of St Jude's, goes round to a friend of St Jude's to ask what sort of chap Jones is, and what bees he has in his bonnet. When you read a work of history always listen out for the buzzing. If you can detect none, either you are tone deaf or your historian is a dull dog. (Carr 1990, p.23)

Carr likens the process of history to deep sea fishing where, to some extent, chance affects what you catch as does the part of the ocean being fished and the kind of tackle used. If you add to that the particular fish you want to catch (and fry) then the problem of history becomes acute. We can lengthen the list: these days you would need to restrict yourself to the prescribed quota as well as taking account of the thinking of those whom you might want to impress or sell your catch to.

Whig history

Whig historians were criticised because:

> they made assumptions about the direction history had taken; namely,
> towards a political system of which they fully approved. Whig history was
> therefore nationalistic, liberal, optimistic, judgmental and written with a
> goal or ideal in mind. (Warren 1999, p.66)

The most damning challenge to this sort of history came from women's
groups who sought to re-write events and clarify the roles women played.
Similar moves took place in race studies where western accounts were seen as
overtly Eurocentric in nature. The case of Mary Seacole is instructive here: she
was a nurse of Afro-Caribbean origin who went to aid stricken soldiers, casu-
alties of the Crimean War. Until recently, history has excluded Seacole whilst
virtually canonising Florence Nightingale for her role in that conflict.

> Miss Nightingale took ship to Scutari; and henceforth, the *beau ideal* of
> professional nursing was not a gentle Mother Superior praying for
> guidance, but a mythical heroine, a Tennysonian creature divinely tall,
> whose look could quell a regiment. (Cohen 1964, p.30)

Not only is Seacole's contribution now clearer but the myth of Nightingale –
the 'Angel with the Lamp' – has had to be redrawn somewhat: the point is,
many women from different social, cultural, class and religious backgrounds
went to the Crimea. Further, Nightingale knew that 'good' nursing had failed
to stem the disaster unfolding at the Scutari hospital. Her work there, valiant
though it was, may have persuaded her that improvements in nursing would
remain an insufficient substitute for medical inefficiency. Subsequent
cover-ups (see Small 1998) by governmental committees fed into an historical
bandwagon which settled on Nightingale as a symbol of progress and
humanity when the true picture – which she tried to convey – was horrifically
different. As a result:

> Her reputation as the merciful angel of Scutari and as the founder of
> secular hospital nursing was no longer an embarrassment to her, it was a
> devilishly cruel and macabre joke at her expense. (Small 1998, p.114)

The drug revolution

The inexorable march of psychiatric science, together with its love-child
psychopharmacology, has been cherished by many psychiatric historians.
Psycho-history provides images of progress which it links to advances in bio-

logical and pharmacological sciences. Such histories are often expressions of what their writers believe the nature of mental illness to be and how it should be treated. Three events will illustrate this: the strange case of Mary Barnes, the introduction, in the 1950s, of Phenothiazine drugs, and the concept of 'psychologisation'.

For years, one of the great therapeutic community fables was that Mary Barnes entered Kingsley Hall, a therapeutic community founded by R.D. Laing in 1965, where she regressed ('went down') into a psychotic state only to re-emerge psychologically healed. The story has been told often but principally in Barnes's own account (Barnes and Berke 1971) written with her helper and psychiatrist, Joseph Berke.

But what actually took place? The answer to that is wrapped up in psychiatry's most widely abused term, schizophrenia. The anti-psychiatric polemic of the Sixties was that psychiatry labelled people with this 'disorder' but that it was really a social construction. Rather than being ill, the schizophrenic is a vulnerable individual who has withdrawn from relationships so as to enter the more primitive reaches of his or her consciousness. When Barnes entered Kingsley Hall, she gradually regressed to literal infancy with Dr Berke cleaning up after her, washing her, and feeding her with a bottle. Mary Barnes would become a celebrated case, an example of recovery from schizophrenia through kinship borne of small community relationships. The case became known as a 'journey through madness' and was the subject of a 1970s London stage play by David Edgar.

In 1978, Professor John Wing published *Reasoning About Madness*. Deliberating on whether madness exists, he made the arresting comment (p.162) that Mary Barnes did not have schizophrenia but that she suffered from hysteria instead, and that Joseph Berke had made a classic diagnostic error. If true, then we have been led astray for some time about what happened at Kingsley Hall. There are even wider implications about what anti-psychiatrists *meant* when using psychiatric terms. For example, in 1970 R.D. Laing and Aaron Esterson published case studies exploring how relationships in families affected the behaviour of schizophrenic family members. Although the subjects involved had been diagnosed independently it is nevertheless striking, reading these case studies, how articulate and organised (in thought and speech) these young schizophrenics are. As in the case of Barnes, one is reminded of how concepts can be either constructed or stretched so as to be made fit for purpose. Having checked psychiatric textbooks for descriptive accounts of both hysteria and schizophrenia, and having matched these against Barnes's history and behaviour, it seems (to me) that she did not have what would normatively pass as schizophrenia. However, my point is that had

Wing not identified this, had it not been flagged up, it would be the anti-psychiatric version that we would now be left with.

My second example I will deal with more comprehensively in Chapter 4. I refer to the introduction of a group of drugs in the Fifties called Phenothiazines, which were proclaimed a 'revolution' and awarded responsibility for the social changes in psychiatric practice then taking place. That these drugs had some positive effects is unquestionable; they were a welcome adjunct to the social reforms in the hospitals and they had a beneficial effect on the symptoms of many patients. That they 'heralded a new dawn', the fission from which all else issued, is doubtful. Yet that's how it seemed to the history writers – at the time mainly doctors – and they used this as the explanatory starting point for the providential expansion of psychiatric medicine. It needs saying that medical history – as a professional discipline – has only been taught in British universities since the 1970s. At the time of psychiatric reforms in the Fifties, and later, 'outsider' accounts were uncommon and so it was relatively easy for these drugs to have mythical status conferred upon them.

My third example comes from Shulamit Ramon (1985) who states that psychoanalysis and behaviourism were positive influences on 'the open door movement' in the 1950s. Collectively, she defined their influence as 'the psychologization of everyday life'. She may be on to something. The problem – as will become plain in Chapter 4 – is that there is scant mention of either psychoanalysis or behaviourism in the writings of open door proponents. This reflects the divide between those wishing to ground practices in psychological theory and those of a more uncomplicated mindset, content to apply workable solutions within hospital systems.

We may surmise that the effects of 'psychologisation' were probably subliminal. 'Psychologisation' is an example of the revisionism by which, following Foucault, forced historical constructs are imposed on events, activities that have resulted in the manufacture of constructs which compete with each other in journals, at conferences and in textbooks. Pagels (1982, p.148) notes how historians view the past as a 'history of ideas', seeing ideas as the mainspring of human action, whereas that which lies within the experiences of those most closely or continuously involved is played down.

Conclusion

> So one could argue that there is no such thing as history in the sense of the
> past at all. All we have is what we write about. Taking this a stage further, it
> has been argued that when we study history, we are merely studying histori-
> ography: the past as seen in the words of historians. (Warren 1998, p.2)

One response to this is to point to primary sources, for example documents
and other written evidence. The problem is that documents are not written
with the aim of enlightening future generations. It is a rare document that
doesn't seek to serve different purposes and it is working out what these might
be that can lead to difficulties. Further, documents also typically relate to small
numbers of people, not reflecting the interests of wider groups. For instance,
apart from some glimpses provided by Barnes and Berke (1971) we know
little about what Kingsley Hall was like. This is true of most therapeutic communities – especially in their formative years – whose descriptions remain the
province of a small number of doctors – Maxwell Jones, David Clark, Dennis
Martin – and are neither corroborated nor contradicted by the many others
who were there.

Thomson (1978, p.90) states that the re-discovery of oral evidence will
bring about fundamental changes in how history is recorded and presented.
How extraordinary it is how little we know about nurses, occupational therapists or *patients*. This is changing now and more voices are being heard especially through qualitative methods of research. Some might challenge the
extent of interpretive overlay which these studies employ: jargon such as
'communalism' and 'permissiveness' didn't come from Henderson staff themselves but were imposed by Rapoport and his team. For others, it is precisely
such theorising that gives this study its readability. As Henry Steele
Commager put it, 'Actually partisanship often adds zest to historical writing:
for partisanship is an expression of interest and excitement and passion, and
these can stir the reader as judiciousness might not' (Commager 1965, p.55).

I certainly hope that the reader will be stirred by what follows here and
galvanised to respond if thought necessary. Whilst I have tried to treat my
material with judicious restraint, I couldn't help but become emotionally
engaged with the various (magnificent) characters and (momentous) events
that came my way. So this book is not a scholastic text but is rather a sequence
of impressions by a vaguely sceptical student of therapeutic communities.
Not, as I have tried to show, that *any* account is essentially value free. I believe
it was Nietzsche who stated that 'ultimately, all argument represents a desire of
the heart'. It seems that that is as viable a base to start from as any other.

References

Barnes, M. and Berke, J. (1971) *Two Accounts of a Journey Through Madness*. London: MacGibbon and Kee.

Butterfield, H. (1931) *The Whig Interpretation of History*. London: Bell.

Carr, E.H. (1990) *What is History?* Harmondsworth: Penguin Books.

Cohen, G.L. (1964) *What's Wrong With Hospitals?* Harmondsworth: Penguin Books.

Commager, H.S. (1965) *The Nature and the Study of History*. Columbus, OH: Charles E. Merrill Books.

Cooper, D. (1970) *Psychiatry and Anti-psychiatry*. St. Albans: Paladin.

Digby, A. (1985) *From York Lunatic Asylum to Bootham Park Hospital*. York: University of York Borthwick Paper 69.

Dingwall, R., Rafferty, A. and Webster, C. (1988) *An Introduction to the Social History of Nursing*. London: Routledge.

Edgar, D. (1979) *Mary Barnes*. London: Methuen.

Foucault, M. (1971) *Madness and Civilisation: A History of Insanity in the Age of Reason*. London: Tavistock Publications.

Halsey, A.H. (1995) *Change in British History*. Oxford: Oxford University Press.

Laing, R.D. and Esterson, A. (1970) *Sanity, Madness and the Family: Families of Schizophrenics*. Harmondsworth: Pelican Books.

Malcolm, E. (1989) *Swift's Hospital: A History of St. Patrick's Hospital, Dublin, 1746–1989*. Dublin: Gill and Macmillan.

Marwick, A. (1982) *British Society Since 1945*. Harmondsworth: Pelican Books.

Marwick, A. (1998) *The Sixties*. Oxford: Oxford University Press.

Nolan, P. (1986) 'Mental nurse training in the 1920s.' *Bulletin of the History of Nursing Group* (Spring) 19–23.

Pagels, E. (1982) *The Gnostic Gospels*. Harmondsworth: Penguin Books.

Porter, R. (1985) 'The patient's view: doing medical history from below.' *Theory and Society 14*, 175–198.

Ramon, S. (1985) *Psychiatry in Britain, Meaning and Policy*. London: Croom Helm.

Rapoport, R. (1960) *The Community as Doctor*. London: Tavistock Publications.

Samuel, R. (1994) *Theatres of Memory*. Verso: London.

Scull, A. (1979) *Museums of Madness*. London: Allen Lane.

Shorter, E. (1997) *A History of Psychiatry*. New York: John Wiley and Sons.

Sigal, C. (1976) *Zone of the Interior*. New York: Thomas Y. Crowell.

Small, H. (1998) *Florence Nightingale: Avenging Angel*. London: Constable.

Thomson, P. (1978) *The Voice of the Past: Oral History*. Oxford: Oxford University Press.

Warren, J. (1998) *The Past and its Presenters*. London: Hodder and Stoughton.

Warren, J. (1999) *History and the Historians*. London: Hodder and Stoughton.

Winch, P. (1958) *The Idea of a Social Science and its Relation to Philosophy*. London: Routledge.

Wing, J.K. (1978) *Reasoning About Madness*. Oxford: Oxford University Press.

Wright, D. (2001) *Mental Disability in Victorian England: The Earlswood Asylum 1847–1901*. Oxford: Clarendon Press.

CHAPTER 1

The Fifties and Sixties

The 1950s were ten years of foreplay.

Germaine Greer (1984)

The 1950s were grim and impoverished. Meat was rationed, the cooking was dreadful...and to keep warm you bundled yourself up in sweaters and hurried from one pathetic electric fire to another. Luxury meant a steak or banana or a cup of genuine coffee.

Al Alvarez (1999)

Part 1: In the Fifties

The country's resources, human and physical, had been consumed by war. Worse, the wartime atmosphere long outlasted its origins: cities had been razed to the ground and housing stocks seriously depleted; in fact, the country was depleted. Bradbury (1993) recalls literary critic Edmund Wilson, who visited Britain in the late Forties, saying that it looked like a defeated power. Marwick (1990) states that the consequences of war continued throughout the period 1945–1957 but that not all of these were negative: economic expansion and technological developments had begun in earnest and there was a sense that attitudes might be changing as well.

As the Fifties proceeded, conformity amongst ordinary people altered; working-class deference was subsiding even if, for most people, change was slow. Writing about this period, playwright John Osborne (see Osborne 1981, 1991) noted the inertia, painting a picture of a tired Britain, broken by two world wars and depression. This was still the Britain of hanging, of theatre and film censorship, as well as a brutal, if hypocritical, homophobia. It was a time of germination, protest and dissolution; that it was also the decade of the hydrogen bomb only added (to the austerity) a growing despair at the prospect of atomic war and potential annihilation.

In the immediate post-war period, demands for change concentrated on social and economic factors (which the Atlee government of 1945 hoped to

17

bring about). Growing commercialism was leading to a falling off in self-denial and a move towards indulgence and 'the good life'. When Prime Minister Macmillan told the British people that 'they had never had it so good' they must have believed him: the Labour Party was duly rejected and the Tories enjoyed victories in four successive elections (1950, 1951, 1955, 1959).

As Lewis observed:

> You can forgive people in the Fifties for their eagerness to believe that the problems of highly industrialised societies had been solved, that capitalism worked and that the industrial revolution was at last delivering the goods for everyone. (Lewis 1978, p.41)

The problem was that a pre-war ethic of thrift and personal conservatism appeared to be giving way to instant gratification (particularly amongst the young) and the beginnings of a new and curious desire to denigrate self-control as oppressive and unwarranted.

Towards the end of the Fifties, unemployment and poverty had begun to diminish albeit both would return to the north and be made worse by the contrast with southern affluence and the growth of expense account living. Property speculation went hand in hand with homelessness and landlords ran rampant, culminating in the horrors of Rachmanism. If, indeed, people had never had it so good, then why, asks Montgomery (1965), was hire purchase on the increase? Hire purchase became a (perilous) solution to the problem of insufficient money chasing an abundance of goods. Hire purchase, enabled by lax government restrictions, was the way out of a difficult impasse.

Women

One might have thought that the war would have had a liberating effect on women but it didn't: pressures to marry young and have families – pushed by advertising's imagery of the nuclear household with a devoted wife at its centre ('OXO gives a meal man appeal') – continued. Most women, apparently, happily gave up their munitions jobs when the war ended and resumed domestic roles. There is some evidence that women, compared to males, tend towards conservatism on both social and personal issues. In 1955, Gorer reported that 53 per cent of men and 73 per cent of women believed that chastity was still important outside of marriage, and whilst 65 per cent of men opined that women enjoyed the physical aspects of sex as much as men, only 51 per cent of women thought so.

In the 1950s, Victorian sexual attitudes still prevailed to some degree but it is difficult to be precise: sexual behaviour is essentially personal and public statements may not match private practice. Neither are the sexual scandals which collapsed the Macmillan government a reliable gauge by which to speculate about the population as a whole. Akhtar and Humphries (2001) have interviewed people who were teenagers at the time, and their data corroborates Gorer's 1950s findings that virginity was still a prized possession, especially amongst females, with courtships a persistent struggle to keep testosterone-driven males at bay. When this failed and pregnancies resulted, this typically meant a hastily arranged marriage: the alternative was to enter a Church of England or Catholic Magdalene House where the baby could be born and given up for adoption.

The conjugal 'rights' of working class males held sway:

> My husband wanted sex every night and it was too much for me. I was tired out after a long day's work and looking after the children. It wasn't enjoyable for me at all. But the advice I got was that the problem was mine and that really I should just do it and pretend to enjoy it or he'd look for it elsewhere. (Akhtar and Humphries 2001, p.175)

These writers paint a grim picture, with women driven to depression by men who see male orgasmic sex as their right. It was a 'right' that would come under increasing attack.

Lost children

The Fifties can be said with some truth to be the (lost) decade of idyllic childhood. Undoubtedly the period has been mythologised into a world where children were safe: it is that period to which people of a certain age look back as being a time when children played outdoors without a care in the world. This 'going out to play' would gradually change as more comfortable homes with good lighting (and televisions) – plus the dangers of speeding cars – began to drive children indoors. In addition, reading to children became popular, probably due to changing attitudes towards child rearing. John Bowlby's (1965) *Child Care and the Growth of Love* became a Fifties best seller and significantly influenced middle-class parenting. It introduced a concept of maternal deprivation which held that, deprived of their biological mothers, children would develop neuroses in later life.

Dr Benjamin Spock advocated liberal regimes of child rearing, advising that mothers trust their instincts and ignore the ancestral sureties of the past. What Spock and Bowlby had in common was the promotion of motherhood as an instinctive, housebound, activity: women's work was bringing up baby, the difference being that there was now a 'right way' to do it. To some extent one sees in the Spock and Bowlby babies of the Fifties the student dissidents and radicals of the Sixties.

Television

The progression from 1950s black and white to 1960s colour television is a metaphor for a period where profound social change seemed imminent. Fifties television was bland: many variety artists refused to appear on it and most of its programmes – despite contemporary nostalgia for *Muffin the Mule* and *The Flower Pot Men* – were stagy and amateurish. Television's social status was low, its relationship to radio that of poor cousin. Although the coronation had been televised in 1952 – watched for the most part on small (purpose bought) nine-inch screens – much persuasion had been needed to convince the establishment to let it be shown. Its televising added to the stature of the BBC, much of whose reputation was bound up in the character of John Reith, its first Director General. 'The Reithian principle, patronising, paternalistic and pig-headed, was that the BBC was a cultural priesthood, diffusing such culture through the community as it thought good for it' (Lewis 1978, p.211).

The choice, it seems, was either to be patronised by the BBC or commercially exploited by US imports. American television was widely (and correctly) perceived as commodified and lacking taste. Not that British television was tasteful, and a more correct comparison might be between insipidness and vulgarity. In America, advertisers had influence over programming so that even serious shows – the documentaries of Edward Murrow for instance – had difficulty surviving at all. In Britain, a more balanced system allowed for better programming and eventually independent, not *commercial*, television began to successfully compete with the BBC.

Anxious times

Some of the most important 20th-century fiction was written in the Fifties. Writers began to explore social, class and human relationships in works like *Animal Farm* and *Look Back in Anger*. These works broke with traditions that had become overly redolent of establishment values: if their attacks on Church, Press and State wore a bit thin this was at least different to what had gone before. Exactly to whom this work appealed is difficult to assess: for the broad mass of people, escaping the drudgery of working-class life probably took precedence over criticising the middle classes. In John Braine's *Room at the Top*, the upwardly mobile Joe Lampton surveys his own social class and derides its complacency and lack of passion. For Lampton, the trick is not to get rid of the class system, but to manipulate it for its own ends; he represents a northern ethic of class resentment, seemingly assuaged by wealth and possessions.

Much of the social ferment of the Fifties however, such as it was, took place in the south with fads and fashions taken up primarily by the middle classes. The Beatniks, for instance, hung out in coffee bars listening to jazz: they considered it cool to be serious and liked to be seen reading books such as Kerouac's (1958) *On the Road*, a kind of testimony to the existentialist's life journey or trip. The beats had their political side too, joining in 'ban the bomb' marches and discussing the profounder implications of politics. Halsey (1995) comments that their dark (gothic) appearance and the heaviness of their discussions reflected the period's futility and pessimism. They were not typical, of course, and were seen by some as eccentric, even figures of fun. But they suggested that the young were no longer controlled by their elders or betters. Although the 1950s were still pretty conformist, young people were increasingly refusing to put up with rules and restrictions. Akhtar and Humphries recall:

> Many dance halls had rules that tightly controlled the dress and behaviour of their customers and more adventurous dances like the jitterbug and the jive were banned in some places. (Akhtar and Humphries 2001, p.36)

Refusal to comply could result in being frogmarched to the door and maybe a clip around the ear to boot. This, though, was about to change: *teenagers* were on the horizon and, before long, would be perceived as ruling the roost. Soon, generation gaps, teenage angst, youth rebellion and juvenile delinquency would abound and older generations began to worry. They need not have done: it was largely a mirage and lacked substance.

> By mid 1959 there were 5,000,000 teenagers in Britain. About 4,000,000 of them (2,000,000 boys and 2,000,000 girls) were at work in business and industry; the other 1,000,000 were either still at school or college (650,000) or in the armed forces (350,000). (Montgomery 1965, p.147)

In other words, most young people were leading ordinary, productive lives, so much so that it becomes difficult to see how 'rebellious youth' got its reputation. Vereker's observations yield some clues:

I think that what first struck me in the late Fifties and early Sixties was what appeared to be the sudden emergence of a distinctive group called teenagers and that my own children were part of that group. Whilst we had passed with as little attention as possible from childhood to adult life, there was now a well publicised body of teenage needs, catered for by special clothes, make-up and magazines. (Vereker 1988, p.141)

The last sentence gives the clue. Differences between the generations were real enough but they were based on superficial changes in fashion, music and so on. Deeper values pertaining to class, ethnicity, religion and education did not significantly alter and there were no unusual interchanges between different classes or social groups. Something that *did* alter was sexual behaviour: in the 1950s, such changes were still only apparent, but movement was afoot here that had long-term implications.

Markets

The young became a lucrative market. With four million of them earning £8 (males) or £6 (females) per week, their buying power was increasing. It is problematic whether variations in youth culture were spontaneous, with mercantilists cashing in, or whether market economies amplified changes to their own ends. Teddy boys are a case in point: their dandy (Edwardian styled) clothes marked them out as attention seekers. Unlike the Beatniks they were a working-class phenomenon, London-based, and probably few in number. They did not constitute a social threat even if there were some clashes with police. In a way, they can be seen as a prototype of today's urban gangs, but mainly, they were colonising a visual style that was less 'top-down' (where fashion houses imposed trends) and more, in George Melly's (1970) phrase, a 'Revolt into Style', a rejection of culture as the prerogative of the few. Now, culture would be popular and, arguably, the consumer became king.

Psychiatry

The post-war years were a catalyst for changes in psychiatric concepts: servicemen returning from battle in varying degrees of psychological distress influenced psychiatric thinking. Medical officers had found themselves in new and different relationships with them; whereas, before the war, class differences might have fed into professional encounters, now military experience was influencing decisions about how best to respond to psychiatric distress. There began an unwillingness to stand superiorly apart and a new determination to gauge soldiers' problems as they saw them. Psychiatry was becoming more multifaceted: as we will see, in Chapter 6, both conservatism and liberalism often go hand in hand, or, from a different perspective, psychiatry's essential conservatism historically gave rise to radicalisms which sought to redress doctor–patient relationships in favour of the patient. As the Fifties progressed, some psychiatrists began to address the need for a broader, sociological approach to mental illness and distress. To that end, they sought to reorganise hospital practice and, in particular, challenge traditional formations of power within them. In some cases, small communities were established where participants could retreat so as to re-examine their lives with a view to obtaining a trauma-free re-entry into society. These innovations in institutional care were one of the more optimistic undertakings of the 1950s and have, with ups and downs, continued to inform mental health practice.

Part 2: In the Sixties

Radicalism was the only game in town.

Anon

Epochs are marked as much by discontinuities from the past, which are perhaps easier to see, than by their implications for the future. That said:

> the attitudes which shaped the Sixties were largely forged during the second world war, with the Beveridge Report of 1942 and the 1944 Education Act as midwife and wet-nurse. (Connolly 1995, p.1)

It is a mythologised Sixties that prevails, a Sixties with none of the pessimism and post-war dreariness which in fact continued to pervade its economic and political climate. Although the 'you never had it so good' ambience implied a nation relatively at ease with itself, to a large extent the good feelings were buttressed by welfarism and a crass consumerism which enabled increasing numbers of young people to buy their way into apparent affluence. Most of these youngsters, of course, had never heard of R.D. Laing or Marcuse, Warhol or existentialism. Most of them would never experience a 'love in' or 'flower power' or other symptoms of the 'new consciousness': these were the playthings of the few. True, it was the broad mass of youth that gave rise to new fashions in music, clothes, hairstyles and language. But only a minority were privy to the burgeoning (and self-conscious) preoccupation with social, political and cultural changes.

Curiously, it remains a problem as to how 'the Sixties' coalesced, how they acquired their revolutionary patina. In his novel *The History Man* (1975) Malcolm Bradbury traces the history of the Kirks, a provincial Sixties couple now living and working in a new university town. It was around this time, says Bradbury, that something happened to Howard and Barbara Kirk, something that switched them from Fifties' provincialism to Sixties' radical chic: the question being:

> What happened? Well, their saliva began to flow faster; everything started to get a new taste. The walls of limitation they had been living inside suddenly began to give way; they both started to vibrate with new desires and expectations. Their timidity, their anger, their irritation slipped, bit by bit, off them, like their old clothes…which they discarded…their manner, their style, their natures freshened. They laughed more and challenged people more…and embarked on ambitious new schemes of sexuality. And what had done this to the Kirks? Well, to understand it…you need to know a little Marx, a little Freud, and a little social history; admittedly, with Howard, you need to know all this to explain anything. You need to know…the state of and the determinants of consciousness, and the human capacity of consciousness to expand and explode. And if you understand these things you will understand why it was that the old Kirks faded from sight and the new Kirks came into being. (Bradbury 1975, pp.22–23)[1]

In a way, being *of* the Sixties also meant that you acquired new idols as well as a capacity to despise old ones: Peter Vansittart tells how he once quoted from Captain Scott's last letters: 'We are showing that Englishmen can still die with a bold spirit, fighting it out to the end… I think this makes an example to Englishmen of the future', and of how this had been piously received when read out to classes in 1935 but that now, in the Sixties, 'audiences assumed I was being sardonic and gave appreciative titters' (Vansittart 1995, p.153) When Vansittart amended the quote to make it seem as if it came from Che Guevara it won respectful applause and not a little awe.

No big causes

In *Look Back in Anger*, Jimmy Porter complains that all the crusades are now spent: a questionable sentiment. As Levin says:

> Less than half a decade later the Sixties were upon us [and] no slogan has ever so entirely falsified so quickly. The decade was littered, from beginning to end, with Causes. (Levin 1972, p.251)

For Levin, the Sixties was a time of change but also of gullibility and Bradbury's depiction of Howard Kirk shows how gullibility invites intellectual pretentiousness (usually wrapped up in a cause) plus derision towards those who disagree. Bradbury's novel is peppered with exchanges showing how difficult it had become to deviate from whatever dominant ideological construct held sway. When Howard attacks a colleague, Henry, as being too attached to established ideas, Henry replies:

> I've stopped wanting to stand up and forge history... And I'm rather sick of the great secular dominion of liberation and equality we were on about then, which reduces, when you think about it, to putting system over people... I don't want to blame anyone now, or take anything off anyone. The only thing that matters for me is attachment to other knowable people, and the gentleness of relationship. (Bradbury 1975, p.171)[1]

Howard snarls:

> Well, that's what we all want, isn't it? Sweetness and light and plenty of Mozart. But we can't have it, and you can hardly sit back and rest on your own record. If that's life, Henry, you're not very good at it, are you? (Bradbury 1975, p.171)[1]

Henry knows that his misfortunes are the sad expressions of the personal life which he's not good at: but he is suspicious of systems which proclaim solutions to what he calls 'the whole sad little comedy of living'. Unfortunately for Henry, the Sixties was Howard's time, the time of isms, ologies, Marx and Coca Cola.

Radical psychiatry

The radical psychiatrists of the Sixties took a complex approach to these issues: R. D. Laing (1960) respected individuals but visualised the family as the negative *source* of how individuals come to perceive their surroundings. Although Laing placed the family above Marxism, as an explanatory mechanism, Howard Kirk greatly admired Laing as one of the radical fountainheads of the age.

However, the Sixties was more mottled than Howard would have us believe. Economic crises persisted well into the Seventies, and disaffection over the Vietnam War raged throughout. Still, disturbances in Britain were muted compared to student revolts in France and Germany. In fact, for the British, most of what we nowadays construe as 'the Sixties' was restricted to a few. Masters notes that:

> Whilst thousands flocked to the capital to smell the air of excitement, hoping the benefits of the new age might be contagious, those actually 'in the swim' numbered a few hundred only, and the small band of achievers were less than fifty individuals. (Masters 1985, p.15)

A lot depends here on what is meant by 'in the swim' but it is probably true that most people looked on as England swung: but they would have been conscious of change; it would have influenced them and they would have *enjoyed* the Sixties, even as a spectator sport.

Women and the Sixties

Fifties women were less liberated than their Sixties counterparts who witnessed advances towards greater autonomy and power. However, whilst a 'women's movement' began to come together, it did not represent women generally. As such, interpreting events becomes difficult as does decoding the hyperbole that goes with the territory.

The counterculture of the 1960s is often assumed to encompass women's liberation. In fact, the counterculture was oversubscribed by men, their chauvinism decked out in radical jargon about the politics of sexual liberation and so on.

> By 1967–68, *Oz* had become the market leader among London's liberated underground publications, dependably delivering images of sexual sadism, obscenity, and theatre-of-cruelty in a riot of polychrome newsprint and psychedelic topography, whilst presenting itself as the subvertor of bourgeois repression. (Caute 1988, p.235)

When the Dialectics of Liberation Conference convened in London in 1967, with most of Britain's radical psychiatrists in attendance, it too was a male event incapable of recognising women's issues. Even when nominally included within the various groups that comprised the anti-bourgeois mentality, women were allotted subservient functions and, ultimately, asserting their status *as women* meant rejecting the 'liberated' roles to which they had been assigned. It is clear that from around 1968–1975 there was stirring a realisation, by women, of themselves as a distinct group:

> It would be hard to express...just what sisterhood meant in early 1970s. It was like falling in love. In fact for many women it *was* falling in love. The love affair was sadly brief but it provided an atmosphere of total trust in which to learn how to think and how to act. (Phillips 1983, p.120)

In *Very Heaven* Sara Maitland says, 'The Fifties are perceived...as the decade of femininity, the Seventies as the decade of women. What happened in the ten years in between that changed that?' (Maitland 1988, p.3). Maitland finds it difficult to be precise about this: the first British National Women's Liberation Conference took place at Oxford in 1970 but what brought it about remains obscure. Says Maitland:

> Looking at my own writing, particularly my fiction, I find in it increasingly both an exaltation of and a lament for the Sixties. Something very extraordinary happened to the world then, and particularly to women, from which we have mercifully not yet recovered... (Maitland 1988, p.3)

In Angela Carter's view:

> There is a tendency to underplay, even to devalue completely the experience of the 1960s, especially for women, but towards the end of that decade there was a brief period of public philosophical awareness that occurs only very occasionally in human history; when, truly, it felt like Year One, when all that was holy was in the process of being profaned and we were attempting to grapple with the real relations between human beings. (Carter 1983, p.70)

Barbara Castle was not in sympathy:

> By the Sixties, attitudes to sex had moved a long way from those prevalent in my pre-war years and I did not like the direction in which the women's movement was turning them. I had no use for the sex war and all the nonsense about encouraging women to believe they could only feel big by making men feel small. As a socialist I wanted to make everyone feel big and I believed you could only liberate women by liberating human beings in general. (in Maitland 1988, p.51)

Castle was probably more representative of women than was 'the women's movement'. Yet numbers are a poor measure of influence and it would be mistaken to underestimate the effects of feminism across a range of indices: many more women now chose to work and/or postpone having families until *they* chose to do so. Legislation on abortion, equal opportunities, divorce and family law increased their autonomy, albeit women continued to be under-represented in Parliament and national politics generally.

Sexual attitudes

Sexual attitudes unquestionably changed in the 1960s. For example, underground magazines proliferated, plying their readers with radical politics laced with a rampant sexuality that verged on the obscene. Richard Neville – editor of *Oz* – stated: 'the weapons of revolution are obscenity, blasphemy and drugs', and some magazines exceeded legal limits before being shut down and, in some cases, their editors sent to jail. These crackdowns indicated apprehension in some quarters and before long the 'new sexuality' and the older 'moralities' would collide.

Regina v Penguin Books Ltd (October 1960)

When Penguin Books published *Lady Chatterley's Lover*, charges were brought under the Obscene Publications Act of 1959. The case is a watershed, not just in its efforts to define pornography but, more so, as a blatant attempt to state what people could or couldn't read. It was a case of social class and sex intertwined. It was Penguin Books who had introduced into Britain good, paperback books at prices most people could afford. Had the Chatterley book been in hardback only, a prosecution would not have been brought. The case has its roots in the dismay felt by some that traditional values were receding and that human behaviour was freeing itself from older social controls.

But it was a single sentence, uttered by the prosecutor, which has come to epitomise the chauvinistic and hypocritical attitudes which pervaded the trial: Mr Mervyn Griffith-Jones's question to the jury: 'Would you like your wife or your servants to read it?'

This was the rub: that the book would foment unrest amongst women and the working classes. Indeed, the case exemplified class consciousness – its links with sexuality, condescension and power. Marvelling at the voice of the trial prosecutor, Kenneth Tynan remarked:

> It exhaled class-consciousness as effortlessly as air. Would the jury wish their servants to read Lawrence's novel? And was it natural for the lady of a great house to run off and copulate with her husband's game keeper ... Leisurely and deadly, the voice hounded Connie Chatterley, a traitress to her class in that she not only enjoyed sex, but enjoyed it with a quasi-peasant. (in Connolly 1995, p.11)

Wheen (1982) says it hardly mattered that the liberal intelligentsia was prepared to testify for the book because the prosecution would have seen such

witnesses as belonging to the establishment 'club' and so immune from cor-
ruption. Wheen quotes the judge:

> You know, once a book goes into circulation it does not spend its time in the
> rarefied atmosphere of some academic institution...it finds its way into the
> bookshops and on to the bookstalls, at 3s 6d a time, into public libraries,
> where it is available for all and sundry. (Wheen 1982, p.93)

After deliberating for three hours the jury found in favour of Penguin Books,
deciding that the riffraff could read the book after all.

Together with the scandals of 1963 (of which the John Profumo case is
the best known) the Chatterley trial ushered in 'the permissive society' with a
bang. Yet whilst it does mark the casting aside of hypocrisy, the prurient sug-
gestiveness of the Profumo scandal seems more akin to our current fascination
with sleaze. In the Sixties, sexuality as a liberating and fulfilling force went
hand in hand with sexuality as a furtive and exploitative exercise. But it is to
the first kind that we look when thinking of the period, a more frivolous side
where, especially amongst the young, the new-found sexuality had an open,
blameless quality about it. However, over time, liberal patterns of sexual
behaviour led to shifting attitudes towards longer term relationships. By the
late Seventies, and certainly by the 1980s, various studies confirmed that
growing numbers of younger and younger people were sexually active and
that this was having a bearing on traditional progressions of courtship and
marriage. The Abortion Act (1967) and The Matrimonial Reform Act (1970)
were testimony to the recognition by the State that regulation of these
changes was required. The effects of the new divorce laws became obvious: in
1965 there were 37,785 divorces in Great Britain but by 1975 the figure had
leaped to 120,552.

Class 1: money, drugs, and rock and roll

Sociologists have habitually depicted teddy boys, punks, rockers and
skinheads as working class with counterculturists portrayed as middle class,
the class which sees itself as responsible for – and having a capacity to alter –
the prevailing social order. Although mods and rockers *appeared* to be a force
to be reckoned with, theirs was a reaction based on the more shallow aspects
of change. Counterculture activists, alternatively, seemed determined to
uncouple themselves from materialism in favour of organic homesteads,
communes, the use of prohibited drugs and whatever might satiate their
craving for personal expression unhindered by capitalist and/or traditional
family restrictions.

But whether *any* of this was directed at genuine or long-term change is uncertain. In 1968, young people were not *that* politically committed. The Beatles sang 'You say you want a revolution', true: but it had little to do with revolution as such. Although much would be said about the radical views of this or that rock group – the Rolling Stones famously – it was hokum (of which Sir Michael Jagger's recent Knighthood is ultimate proof). Rather was rebellion limited to 'free' expressions of the 'spirit' and an endless celebration of 'the new'; the Sixties should have lasted forever, as Sara Maitland wanted them to, because they brought a sense – but that was all it was – of liberation and kinship. Like all feelings, it felt real at the time and when the Beatles sang 'All You Need is Love' to the biggest satellite audience in history, it felt as if it *could* be true. David Caute captures the sense well:

> The rock festivals satisfied hungers which were both communitarian and vaguely mystical. Despite the frenetic music, young people passed joints around with love and tenderness, not unlike a Quaker meeting waiting for the spirit. (Caute 1988, p.39)

We shouldn't be surprised, therefore, to find that illicit drugs permeated the anti-psychiatric movement now coming on stream. We know from Clancy Sigal's *Zone of the Interior* (1976) that the character meant to be R.D. Laing frequently uses LSD, as do his clients. And he was not alone. Says Caute:

> Berke, a prophet of the counterculture, explained that the Appolonian culture of the West (rational, materialistic, repressed, straight) feared the Dionysian ethos (emotional, hedonistic, communal – and curved). Marijuana and hashish, he said, were medically harmless and much easier to abandon than opiates, tobacco or alcohol. (Caute 1988, p.44)

Dangerous views, given that both Laing and Joseph Berke were medically qualified and likely to be taken seriously. However, the times protected them and whereas today medical advocacy of illegal drugs would incur legal problems, the horrors of heroin addiction were as yet unknown and 'doing your own thing' still had a lot of currency.

Class 2: work, sex and study

Increased educational provision, at both secondary and university levels, began to rework traditional class divisions. Old 'heavy' industry was in a downward spin and newer service 'industries' multiplied: to resource these, technocratic and consumer-oriented personnel were needed and they required training. For the first time, working-class youngsters went to university (or polytechnics) and these now expanded in number. However, post-war governments had also introduced division into the secondary school system. An 'eleven plus' examination earmarked children for either grammar schools or 'non academic' secondary modern schools. Whilst some grammar school children were working class, most of the latter had to settle for the non academic. Left-wing writers were naturally furious and pamphlets flew thick and thin. Some of these idealised working-class people as seekers after knowledge and truth and when the Open University began in 1969 it was anticipated, with scorn in some places, that it would become the 'cloth cap college'. Nothing of the kind happened and the first batches of graduates were from the middle classes, especially teachers. Richard Hoggart observed that working-class people in higher education were:

> exceptional, in their nature untypical of working-class people; their very presence at summer schools, at meetings of learned societies, courses at lectures, is a result of a moving away from the landscape which the majority of their fellows inhabit without much apparent strain. (Hoggart 1957)

Arthur Marwick sees things much the same way:

> When it came to life chances members of the working class were still at a disadvantage compared with all the rest of society. Individual members might move upwards but conditions within the working class, not excluding working class attitudes themselves, discouraged educational aspiration. (Marwick 1990, pp.43–44)

By the late 1960s, new universities were up and running with their spanking new departments of sociology and their very own versions of Howard Kirk. This gave the appearance of radical change and newness but it would be many years yet before the universities would be open virtually to anyone and this, of course, has brought its own problems.

Academia

By 1968, the universities were in uproar: beginning in London but quickly spreading, the trouble was lack of student representation on administrative bodies. This surely was an excuse, though, and student protests and 'sit ins' soon followed upon any issue for which a smidgen of grievance could be generated. Discussing a student leader at Essex University, Caute recalls:

> During the summer David Triesman committed his energies to the interna-
> tional insurrection: in particular the American scene, confiding to New
> Left Review some strategic thoughts... What we should do, wrote
> Triesman, is if the situation were to arise again, would be to behave as pro-
> vocatively as necessary and so effectively sanction the university to the
> extent that they *need* to use force, probably the police. The aim, Triesman
> explained, was to combat 'the whole nauseating apparatus' by which uni-
> versities turned out new generations of capitalist managers. (Caute 1988,
> p.305)

Examinations were selected as especially oppressive and in some places
students reconstituted themselves as a 'free university' with their own
anti-rules and procedures: given the hilariousness of this it is perhaps strange
that a fair number of lecturers aligned themselves with the students and
signed endless petitions in support. Noel Annan (1999) notes that university
authorities were seen as either insensitive to reasonable student demands or
vacillating in their dealings with the militants. Annan believed that the unrest
did the universities harm.

The anti-university

Established in 1967, London's Anti-University provided courses on practically anything to which one could be anti: Dr Joseph Berke, still involved in
therapeutic communities, lectured on anti-hospitals and anti-families and his
opening line was, 'How can we discuss how we can discuss what we want to
discuss?' It appears he didn't get very far with this although others did: one
professor, attempting to demolish power relationships in education, refused
to teach at all. These events typified the anti-institutional temper of the times
and few walks of life escaped its radical glare. David Cooper, founder of Villa
21, a therapeutic community for psychotic people (see Chapter 7), extended
his hatred of families – for him, *the* cause of psychiatric distress – to educational systems. Cooper believed that persecution was widespread but that a
possible way out was through psychoanalysis provided it too wasn't misused:

> All this relates very closely to the situation of young people battling to free
> themselves into their own futures as distinct from those vicariously and
> lovingly prescribed for them by parents and teachers. (Cooper 1971,
> pp.74–75)

In his view, love for children was a pretext by which parents 'saved' themselves. Children become entangled in parental projections which are part of

each generation feeding off the next. Further, if one can not alter one's parents, then one can at least try to alter one's teachers: the problem being that if teachers are compliant with this, educational systems will censure them:

> The answer is to…aim at as massive a drop out of teachers and students as possible to the point of stopping, in concert with similar movements in other institutions, the operations of one's particular school or college as finally and as decisively as possible. (Cooper 1971, pp.75–76)

Cooper adored London's Anti-University: it was backed by the same people behind his Dialectics of Liberation Conference (see Cooper 1968), the showpiece of Sixties radical psychiatry. However, it would be wrong to see radicalised psychiatry as idiosyncratic: the definitive expression of anti-educational rage was a 1968 film called *If* produced by Paramount Pictures and directed by Lindsay Anderson. Set within a public school, its final scene erupts into violence with pupils gunning down the ruling clique of the school.

Reviewing the Sixties

The question is whether we should view the Sixties as:

> an insubstantial bubble of jollity which did more harm than good [Mrs Thatcher's view] or the symptom of a new national pride which did not last long enough. (Masters 1985, p.32)

The counterculture would, in fact, be short-lived, being quickly appropriated by commercial interests. Initially, a New Left critique highlighted its crass commercialism and superficiality whilst later, the Right castigated its libertarianism as the begetter of a (grossly immoral) social and family disintegration. A great deal rests on perception. It's true that change brought advantages but it also brought costs: faster cars and bigger aeroplanes but more pollution and deteriorating roads; better medicine but increasing costs; innovations in psychiatric practice but with the anxieties and deficiencies of 'care in the community'.

For Vansittart, the nation had found, after the war, unsuspected reserves of being and a changing, but still firm, identity: 'I felt that we now had not only the will but also the apparatus for a more humane attitude towards crime, health, sex, women and children, colour, other countries' (Vansittart 1995, p.101).

Support for this was the growing concern about third world issues, the abolition of the death penalty (in 1965) and the setting up of the Race Relations Board the same year. Conscription had gone by 1960 and homosexual law reform was also taking place. Of course, these were matters of contention and homosexual law reform was especially disputatious. One might have expected psychiatry to be in the vanguard of reforming attitudes towards homosexual behaviour. Not so: in fact psychiatry was divided about it with behaviourists continuing to 'treat' it until about 1967 (Rogers 1999). Reflecting on this, psychiatrist David Cooper commented:

> One illuminating bit of the horror story is the diagnosis and treatment of homosexuals by aversion methods. Men who, the psychiatrists complain, are complaining of homosexual wishes have a gadget attached to their penises that measures the strength of erection by the blood volume in the penis. They are shown a series of nude men interspersed with a series of nude women. When they respond to the nude men they are given an electric shock, when they respond to the nude women they are given the reward of a non-shock. (Cooper 1971, p.114)

Today, many of these gay men believe that such 'treatments' ruined their lives (see D'Silva 1996).

In general, resistance to changes in sexual behaviour persisted in the form of objections that recreational sex was destroying loving relationships. There seemed to be a difficulty recognising that the two could go together, that people could manage their sexuality at different levels and degrees of intimacy depending on who they were with, and when and where.

Ending up

Halsey (1995) traces developments from the Sixties as a series of 'tentatively accumulated social bargains' where pragmatism and common sense fostered a consensus about certain norms such as decency, the law, custom and practice, and fair play coupled with scepticism about ideology or conviction politics. Those who govern survive challenges to the status quo by conceding and assimilating the various demands of the excluded and disadvantaged, 'always provided that incorporation has accepted the limitation of not seriously challenging established privileges and rights of property' (Halsey 1995, p.3).

This argument was later re-applied (Baruch and Treacher 1978) to psychiatry to show how orthodox practice emasculates radical ideas which challenge its practices. In the succeeding chapters we will see examples of this: progress occurring in fits and starts, sudden bursts of innovation coupled with rearguard actions, conflicts between theory and practice and the problematic disentangling of argument from rhetoric.

If the Fifties was about austerity and anxiety, as the Sixties unravelled, austerity waned and anxiety began to be explained as *experience*: the problem was now set out less as 'there is anxiety' and more 'I am anxious'. But this individualism must be reconciled with the way in which established groups retain power by alternatively assimilating elements from their critics whilst discarding some of their own less precious attributes. In the case of therapeutic communities, we shall witness their struggle to reconcile their autonomy within corporate demands about accountability, as well as manage debates about the balances (and bargains) to be struck between therapists and patients – and the organisational and personal risks involved for both sides.

Note

1. From *The History Man* by Malcolm Bradbury (1975). London: Secker and Warburg. Copyright © Malcolm Bradbury Estate (1975). Reproduced with permission of Curtis Brown on behalf of Malcolm Bradbury Estate.

References

Akhtar, M and Humphries, S. (2001) *The Fifties and Sixties: A Lifestyle Revolution*. London: Boxtree.

Alvarez, A. (1999) *Where Did it All Go Right?* London: Richard Cohen Books.

Anderson, L. (1968) *If.* London: Paramount Pictures.

Annan, N. (1999) *The Dons: Mentors, Eccentrics and Geniuses*. London: Harper Collins.

Baruch, G. and Treacher, A. (1978) *Psychiatry Observed*. London: Routledge and Kegan Paul.

Bowlby, J. (1965) *Child Care and the Growth of Love*. Harmondsworth: Penguin Books.

Bradbury, M. (1975) *The History Man*. London: Secker and Warburg.

Bradbury, M. (1993) *The Modern British Novel*. Harmondsworth: Penguin Books.

Braine, J. (2001 re-issue) *Room at the Top*. London: Arrow.

Carpenter, H. (2001) *The Angry Young Men: A Literary Comedy of the 1950s*. London: Allen Lane, The Penguin Press.

Carter, A. (1983) 'Notes from the front line.' In M. Wandor (ed) *On Gender and Writing*. London: Pandora Press.

Castle, B. (1988) 'No kitchen cabinet.' In S. Maitland (ed) *Very Heaven: Looking back at the 1960s*. London: Virago Press.

Caute, D. (1988) *Sixty-Eight: The Year Of the Barricades*. London: Hamish Hamilton.

Connolly, R. (1995) *In the Sixties*. London: Pavilion Books.

Cooper, D. (1968) *The Dialectics of Liberation*. Harmondsworth: Penguin Books.

Cooper, D. (1971) *Death of the Family*. London: The Penguin Press.

D'Silva, B. (1996) 'When gay meant mad.' *Independent on Sunday* 4 August, 8–11.

Gorer, G. (1955) *Exploring English Character*. London: Cresset Press.

Greer, G. (1984) *The Late Clive James*. London: Channel Four Television.

Halsey, A.H. (1995) *Change in British Society from 1900 to the Present Day* 4th edn. Oxford: Oxford University Press.

Hoggart, R. (1957) *The Uses of Literacy*. London: Chatto and Windus.

Kerouac, J. (1958) *On the Road*. London: Andre Deutsch.

Laing, R.D. (1960) *The Divided Self*. London: Tavistock Publications.

Levin, B. (1972) *The Pendulum Years: Britain and the Sixties*. London: Pan Books.

Lewis, P. (1978) *The Fifties*. London: Heinemann.

Maitland, S. (1988) *Very Heaven: Looking Back at the 1960s*. London: Virago Press.

Marwick, A. (1990) *British Society Since 1945*. Harmondsworth: Penguin Books.

Masters, B. (1985) *The Swinging Sixties*. London: Constable.

Melly, G. (1970) *Revolt into Style: The Pop Arts in Britain*. London: Allen Lane, The Penguin Press.

Montgomery, J. (1965) *The Fifties*. London: George Allen and Unwin Ltd.

Osborne, J. (1981) *A Better Class of Person*. London: Faber and Faber.

Osborne, J. (1991) *Almost a Gentleman*. London: Faber and Faber.

Phillips, A. (1983) 'Two steps forward, one step back?' In M. Wandor (ed) *On Gender and Writing*. London: Pandora Press.

Rogers, L. (1999) 'Gay cure therapy offered on NHS.' *The Sunday Times* 20 June.

Sigal, C. (1976) *Zone of the Interior*. New York: Thomas Y. Crowell.

Vansittart, P. (1995) *In the Fifties*. London: John Murray.

Vereker, P. (1988) 'From emancipation to liberation.' In S. Maitland (ed) *Very Heaven: Looking Back at the 1960s*. London: Virago Press.

Wheen, F. (1982) *The Sixties*. London: Century Publishing.

CHAPTER 2

The Ways of Hospital Life

The first aim of the hospital should be to do no harm.

Florence Nightingale (1860)

A dependable culture

Reviewing psychiatric hospital life in the 1950s, David Clark observed that: 'The small staff preserved order, prevented escapes, and saw that the patients were adequately fed and clothed' (Clark 1964, p.2). Clark went on to paint a picture of a well-ordered and intricately woven social fabric where patients and staff became interdependent whilst still maintaining their relative institutional roles. For example, patients became an important part of the work force; there arose over time what Bateman and Dunham (1948) called an 'employee culture', one of whose effects was to work against the possible discharge of the patients concerned. Conditions of work and 'treatment' were typically drab and intolerable, an ironic counterpoint to the beauty of the physical surroundings of most hospitals. The general sense is of uninterested and apathetic nursing and medical functionaries resigned to their (self-imposed) world of locked doors and jangling keys, doing their best to keep the custodial ship afloat.

Both medical and nursing education were, at the time, trainings in that they provided students with strict classifications of clinical conditions based in large part on biology and genetic inheritance. Maxwell Jones castigated the pseudoscientific emphasis of academic psychiatry and complained that his own training had been insensitive to the role played by patients: human relations, from the perspective of the psychiatric curriculum was, as yet, an undiscovered dimension. According to H.V. Dicks:

> the content and slant of medical education was calculated to blunt the fine edge of human sensibilities in favour of 'scientific objectivity' in the very years when a young person is seeking his identity and hence for models among his teachers and leaders. (Dicks 1967, p.1134)

Younger doctors appear to have taken refuge from the boredom of hospital routines by attending outpatient departments where they might get a chance to practise some individual psychotherapy. But whatever the enthusiasm for change amongst junior medical personnel, change overall was effectively curtailed by senior ward nursing staff who – with some magnificent exceptions – proved recalcitrant and doggedly unwilling to look to the future.

Physical treatments

The introduction of physical treatments such as insulin coma therapy and electrical convulsion therapy heightened the morale of hospital staff; at last they had something to do and many began to see themselves as more than mere custodians. Clark (1964) called this sudden hive of activity 'furor therapeuticus'.

Over time, however, physical treatments became ends in themselves and their excessive and ill-considered use provoked inquiries into their merits. Bourne (1953) had begun to question the efficacy of insulin therapy showing that if it *was* effective, this had little to do with its physiological properties and more to do with the specialised milieu in which the treatment was given. This was an area of confusion, mistaking positive outcomes as a function of treatment when, in fact, such outcomes stemmed from the intensity attending the treatment's implementation. For example, having studied the use of intravenous acetylcholine to treat neuroses, it was concluded, 'It is clear that the curative property lies not in the drug administered but in some other aspects of the total therapeutic regime' (Hawkins and Tibbetts 1956, p.51).

Although physical treatments would continue to be used, as the Fifties proceeded the 'total therapeutic regime' became more relevant in terms of patient well-being. Drawing upon the WHO Report (1953) (of which he was part author) Thomas Rees, medical superintendent of Warlingham Park Hospital, stated that:

> The most important single factor in the efficacy of the treatment given in a mental hospital appears to be an intangible element which can only be described as its atmosphere. (Rees 1957, p.310)

What was beginning to be recognised was that whatever the value of physical treatments, what was also needed was an appraisal of how the social milieu influenced treatments overall. Whilst the new psycho-drugs were being over praised as having revolutionised the social worlds of patients, less recognition attended the optimism which the new treatments bred *in the staff*, leading them to hold more positive outlooks, and thus enhancing their working lives and the lives of their patients.

War

Growing recognition that social factors were implicated in the aetiology of mental disturbance went hand in hand with psychiatrist's experiences of the Second World War. The traditional concept of mental illness as inborn was dislodged by war-induced trauma which many soldiers were experiencing. Obviously, it was unhelpful to assume that all of these soldiers were biologically predisposed to mental breakdown. For many of them, their war experiences were central to what ailed them. Something needed to be done about this. Following the war, Bion's (1961) group experiments at Northfield Military Hospital showed that interpersonal relationships could influence behaviour and this was only one of a series of ideas that took hold at Northfield. Whiteley (1979) believed that psychiatrists turned to 'social constructs' as a way forward because they had little in the way of physical treatments to fall back on. However, as we have seen, since the 1930s there had been treatments galore and these were joined – in some cases supplanted – in the 1950s by the Phenothiazine drugs, which were said to diminish psychotic symptoms without sedation.

In truth, psychiatry would progress along two fronts simultaneously, encouraging new developments in social therapies but adhering also, perhaps more enthusiastically, to its physical (drug and electric) treatments. Over time, the drugs grew in stature and reputation, being seen by many as *the* yardstick against which psychiatric progress would be measured, a propaganda which continues. Dratcu (2000), for instance, identifies the emergence of psychosocial therapies as well as the move to community psychiatry as due to their introduction. The truth, as Bennet notes, is more complicated:

> From the middle 1950s the new pharmaco-therapies played their part (but) had less effect on patients in hospitals where therapeutic optimism and organisational change had preceded their use. (Bennet 1978, p.210)

The formation of the NHS also brought about a greater social awareness within the mental hospitals and a need to take account of public attitudes. Before the NHS little attention had been paid to public relations between hospitals and community: now the Ministry of Health stressed the necessity of good public relations (Hawker 1985) and several medical superintendents became adept at reassuring local communities about changes, for example unlocking doors, then taking place in their hospitals.

The problem was that, until the 1950s, the hospitals were largely moribund (and many would continue that way). There were lots of good ideas around but transferring theory into practice is never easy and often years can elapse before one becomes the other. Hinshelwood states that:

> Most psychologists, sociologists and biologists sit with their backs to each other. And in the middle of this uncomfortable three-way see-saw are doctors and therapists trying to keep their balance. This is the acrobatic position we work in a therapeutic community. It is the glorious privilege of academics to know that they are on the track of knowing everything. It is the humble gloom of the practitioner to know that nearly everything remains uncertain and paradoxical. (Hinshelwood 1983, p.167)

We shall see elements of this in Chapters 4 and 5 when a perturbed nursing staff come face to face with the problems of unlocking hospital doors as well as different aspects of therapeutic community practice.

Bierer had earlier stated that:

> It is a mistaken ambition to want to appear scientific at the expense of our patient's health. We may attempt to use scientific methods for the investigation of psychological diseases. The practical application cannot yet follow preconceived plans or our present day methods of science. It is an art; and art does not follow the laws of differentiation but those of conceiving things as a whole. (Bierer 1940, p.937)

And people's concepts of psychological diseases differed: so naturally did their perceptions in respect of enabling mentally ill people to acquire more self-direction. The nurses, for instance, typically saw the darker side of giving ('potentially malevolent') patients more autonomy. The new social psychiatry was not without its medical critics either. Disdain sometimes met proposed changes to the primary position of the physician. In his introduction to Maxwell Jones's book *Social Psychiatry* (1952) Aubrey Lewis displays a curiously half-hearted praise: the book, says Lewis, possesses 'interesting ideas which may yet prove to be worthwhile' and the sense is that whilst these ideas might make a worthy conference paper, their use as 'treatments' is somewhat doubtful. An air of condescension often pervades orthodox psychiatry's responses to unorthodox or radical innovations. Alternatively, as we shall see, responses can involve elements of assimilation whereby would-be radicalism is shorn of its 'offensive' dimensions and made safe in the hands of the many.

Social research of institutions

As well as recognition of the effects of war, studies of institutional life were coming on stream, particularly in America, and proving to be very significant. For example, Stanton and Schwartz's *The Mental Hospital* provided a method for examining a hospital as a 'total culture'. Observing patterns of relationships between staff and the kinds of internal and external assumptions that governed their actions, Stanton and Schwartz showed that problems often stemmed from 'the organisation of decision making', specifically the absence of arrangements by which difficulties could be identified or where the conditions which brought them about could be dealt with. Appraisal was 'inaccurate, poorly directed, hit or miss, and unnecessarily painful. The emotional cost of this was heavy' (Stanton and Schwartz 1954, p.405).

Patient's symptoms were directly related to the organisation of the hospital, a highly developed and specialised apparatus when pursuing its manifest purposes, but only of benefit to patients when these processes worked smoothly. In Britain, Rees (1957) called for the introduction of group discussion as a possible antidote to this tension and worsening atmosphere. Stanton and Schwartz (1954) had also noted high staff turnover, with nurses leaving because of emotional problems directly related to the work. Nurses were particularly upset by threats of change to their methods of working. It was Stanton and Schwartz's contention that communications between staff were skewed because of how they perceived their designated roles and the institution's formal and informal expectations of them. Whereas excitement or distress in patients had hitherto been seen as indicative of mental illness, in the Stanton and Schwartz study such reactions often correlated positively with distresses embedded in the hospital's administration. When staff disagreements resolved themselves through discussion, then distress diminished in patients even when the latter were unaware of the discussions.

One of the problems with these early American studies (see also Caudill 1958) is that they were carried out in quite small, specialised units. Belknap (1956) provided the first description of a (much larger) mental hospital and his findings more accurately mirrored the kinds of problems facing the average British mental hospital. Belknap was especially interested in length of stay, and showed that whilst staff (unlike patients) could be transitory there existed a nucleus of staff who spent their entire lives working in the hospital. These were the people who provided the cultural continuity of hospitals. Stanton and Schwartz (1954) had also observed this as had Rees who wrote of:

> a hard core of old hands, consisting of male nurses, artisans, senior female nurses, senior doctors and sometimes medical superintendents, who appear, like the long-stay patients, to go on for ever. These are the people ...who are responsible for the pattern and culture of the hospital...for handing on its traditions. (Rees 1957, p.310)

Belknap (1956) further showed how the hierarchical structure of hospitals intertwined with the belief systems of these 'lifers' and, through careful observations and astute interviews, how these two dimensions coalesced over generations into a bastion of resistance to anything smacking of newness or difference.

Goffman's dynamic

Although Erving Goffman's work (1961) is accused by some of being anecdotal it was precisely his style which gave it its creative edge and power. His writing was incisive: brilliantly, he captured the destructive processes which institutions wrought in their inmates: this was no plodding, methodologically grounded analysis but a tour de force, full of invective against the totalitarian proclivities of institutions, including hospitals. In particular, Goffman showed how mental institutions develop psychological distance from their environments, how they evolve inclusive social roles and how these act to inhibit behaviours not in keeping with the norms that constitute those roles. When practices become institutionalised, new and circumscribed sets of rules spring up and these take precedence over the everyday rules and norms which govern societies. In the case of mental hospitals, it becomes an imperative to initiate newcomers (especially patients) into this circumscribed world and it is here that processes of 'social stripping' – for example, admission procedures – remove any vestiges of social identity as the person assumes their new patient identity.

Goffman's appeal lay in his capacity to capture the capricious and oppressive appetites of institutions and how these shape individuals within them. Whilst a number of literary minded practitioners (in Britain) were captivated by his writing – the English playwright Alan Bennett speaks highly of Goffman – contemporary British social psychiatric literature took a more pragmatic turn. Martin described how psychiatric in-patient life resulted in apathy, dependence and loss of individuality and he named this 'institutionalisation'. Interestingly, he pointed out that 'once in hospital the patient quickly becomes absorbed into its highly organised life' (Martin 1955, p.1189).

Becoming absorbed was often the prerequisite by which recovery was judged as in: 'he gives no trouble, doctor, he is very co-operative'. Barton (1976) deployed vivid examples from case notes: 'remains uncommunicative, withdrawn and unoccupied', 'dull depressed and solitary', to show how these reflected an *imposed* hospital order which had become virtually impermeable to outside agencies. Barton detailed how the social fabric of hospitals *facilitated* deterioration, but it is interesting how his descriptions also match the criteria for schizophrenic diagnoses. In other words, the kinds of criteria upon which schizophrenic diagnoses were based could actually be an outcome of long-term hospitalisation. Barton had compared the behaviours of newly admitted patients to later behaviours so as to illustrate how their deterioration had come about in this way. However, he was a doctor and so unable to forego the medical impulse to categorise: hence his re-formulation of institution-alisation into the medically sounding syndrome 'institutional neurosis'. He did this, he said:

> because it promotes the syndrome to the category of a disease, rather than a process, thereby encouraging us to understand, approach and deal with it in the same way as other diseases. (Barton 1976, p.2)

He was opposed to analyses which relied on social theory:

> Criticism of specific examples of actions by named people which are thought to be detrimental are best avoided in general meetings. Unrealistic demands and politics must also be deterred. (Barton 1976, p.50)

Nevertheless, Barton's study was challenging and it initiated social activities in many wards and units across the country. It exposed many shortcomings, especially the negativity of nursing regimes and the pervasive morbidity of many hospitals wards. In many ways, entering a mental hospital in Britain in the 1950s was to experience at first hand a dispiriting return to an earlier, almost Dickensian, age.

The size of the problem

When Gerda Cohen (1964) published her survey, England still had many large mental hospitals, at least 30 of them containing more than 2000 patients. Nobody had planned these human ant-heaps but for a variety of reasons they had rapidly grown. The question of why they became overpopulated is heavily contested (see Jones 1972 and Scull 1979 for opposing viewpoints). The debate hinges on such things as societal intent, for instance Foucault's (1971) notion – now becoming discredited – that emergent capitalism sought to exclude the mad since they were unproductive. Or, alternatively, that an altruistic, Victorian, resolve set out to provide civilised accommodation for less able pauper-lunatics. A great deal depends on who you read. Both Kathleen Jones and Andrew Scull embody different approaches to writing history. Jones represents that history where 'the facts' – in the form of primary sources – 'speak for themselves': Scull is a more 'interpretive' historian, the kind who constructs grand theories of *why* things happened. In effect, he ploughs intentions into history, which is not to say that the Jonesian perspective lacks interpretation. Indeed, her steady exposition of Victorian 'good will', coupled with a curious avoidance of the asylum's bad points, is as intentioned as any other account.

Demise

It is quite sobering to think that the demise of the mental hospitals was anticipated only 60-odd years from their construction. In March 1961, Enoch Powell, Minister for Health, addressed the National Association for Mental Health and announced the elimination of these hospitals as they then existed. He said:

> This is a colossal undertaking, not so much in the new physical provision which it involves, as in the sheer inertia of mind and matter which it requires to be overcome. There they stand, isolated, majestic, imperious, brooded over by the gigantic water tower and chimney combined, rising unmistakable and daunting out of the countryside – the asylums which our forefathers built to express the notions of their day. (Powell 1961, pp.4–10)

Not everyone wanted the transformation, although as time passed, dragging one's heels was no longer suggestive of resistance but could now be seen in more complex ways. Some feared that new proposals for departments of psychiatry within district general hospitals would cream off treatable, acute, cases leaving long-term term patients to fester in the old mental hospitals. Showing an astonishing prescience about what would soon be called 'community care', Gerda Cohen wrote:

> Beyond a few exceptional cities, there is fragmentary liaison between the agents responsible for after care. Hostels for convalescents are few and maldistributed. Local authority plans for the development of health welfare services in the next ten years do nothing to allay fears that some authorities will skimp on provision for the mentally ill. (Cohen 1964, p.142)

Of course, decanting patients from hospitals to community became a slow (if sure) process and it was only when it quickened that Cohen's predictions manifested themselves. The anti-social conduct of some patients – now deprived of shelter and sustenance – became acute over time and increasingly embarrassing to the Department of Health. In the meantime, progress of sorts was made for those continuing to live within the hospitals. The Phenothiazine drugs were improving the lives of some; physical restraints were becoming a thing of the past and the food improved somewhat. Peculiarly, catatonic patients disappeared, a disappearance that is hard to credit: Professor Alec Jenner wonders if this type of schizophrenia was perhaps caused by an unknown virus, as was the pandemic encephalitis lethargica, new cases of which have not been reported since 1930. Or could it have been straightforward susceptibility to the new drugs in a way which differed from other forms of schizophrenia? Many other types of patients were also said to be benefiting from the new drugs, being less prone to mood swings and/or aggressive behaviour. Not that the absence of symptomology is an indication of well-being. Observing the post-Phenothiazine calm of some of the wards which she visited, Gerda Cohen characterised it as an 'uncanny torpor': 'Instead of madmen in rags, you observe permed, greyish, creatures in pinafores, embroidering egg cosies. The horror has all been ironed out' (Cohen 1964, p.143).

Accounting for the hard-heartedness which must have underpinned the staff's inability to see this is difficult. Certainly their belief that patients don't experience distress in quite the same way the rest of us do is pertinent. For example, when Cohen asked a psychiatrist if mental patients suffer, he replied, 'If they did, they wouldn't be there; they would have co-operated in getting better and leaving' (Cohen 1964, p.145).

This 'inability to suffer' notion is quite old. Porter observes that in the 18th century it was common to think of the lunatic as an animal:

> Semi-naked, filthy, hirsute, often chained or caged and tamed with whips – lunatics in Swift's age were handled very much like animals. (Porter 1990, p.43)

For years after they were built, it was not considered necessary to heat asylums, or install glazed windows, the thinking being, at the time, that lunatics were insensitive to cold. Clearly, the mad had come to be seen as separate from humanity, as having somehow lost the capacity for reason and feeling.

Cohen's hospital excursion in the Sixties showed that little had changed. In one hospital, whilst visiting the 'back blocks' which housed 'the chronics', she noted that the deterioration in standards (from the acute wards) became palpable. Whilst she was upset by the sight of five men 'being undressed and bundled into five grubby bath tubs alongside each other', the charge nurse informed her this was not a problem since: 'They don't know'. In the same hospital Cohen visited the 'Greyhound traps', the only unlocked doors in this hospital. Behind these doors, patients sat on the lavatory and the doors were named from the fact that the patients remained visible, top and bottom, to the watching nurses. These patients were the 'irremediables'.

Such deplorable conditions were observed by others. When Professor John Wing (1970) investigated three hospitals in South East England, he found that, in one, less than half the women had their own outdoor clothes, less than a quarter their own toothbrushes and few possessed any of the intimate paraphernalia considered part and parcel of everyday life. Although Wing observed, towards the close of his tour, that some distribution of tooth-brushes and other items had occurred, he doubted that this would last and believed that matters would slide when he had gone.

Of course, as Goffman would say, forfeiting one's clothing means losing one's identity. In fact, wearing hospital clothing was standard practice for any long-term patient and especially when their families lost interest. Nurses made some effort to dress females appropriately but even here the clothes would, by and large, have an odd look about them. The men looked even more odd with their trousers habitually half way up their ankles and jackets either ludicrously oversized or uncomfortably tight.

Pinpointing responsibility for all of this was a fruitless task: it was asserted that dressing patients in good clothes would only result in their making them dirty and thus requiring them to be changed, so what was the point? Others asserted that patients could not have their own clothes because there was nowhere to store them: it was hard enough to get the required number of beds into overcrowded wards without having to include wardrobes. According to this view, nurses are governed by chronic overcrowding and unable to do much about it. The circumstances *were* difficult but the staff had become so ensnared by the conditions that it becomes hard to work out cause and effect. Over time, people simply 'made do' with the depressing conditions, becoming resigned to them and slipping into an interminable torpor. Many patients of the period had a greyish pallor about them and a listlessness that wasn't helped by being indoors all the time; and when they were allowed out, it was usually under very controlled conditions. As Cohen reports, 'the frail or dim-witted spend their lives indoors, surrounded by beautiful countryside. Once a day, they are let out for an "airing" in their enclosure' (Cohen 1964, p.165). Staff also liked to congregate indoors because they saw their role as containment and this is always more difficult to ensure in the open.

Separation and governance

These conditions resembled how medieval fiefdoms must have operated. At the head sits the medical superintendent, hampered only by the occasional missive from his hospital management committee. His writ runs the length and breath of all that he surveys: he is the Duke in his domain. Beneath the head (medical superintendent) sit the heads of the male and female hospital sides, matron and chief male nurse respectively, two chieftains who generally 'go their own way', only occasionally meeting or even communicating with each other. Beneath them are the sisters and charge-nurses with their propri-etary jurisdiction over their wards: these are the first rung on the authoritarian ladder to which all minions must needs obey. In the main, this is the situation that continued, with growing abatement, until the late 1970s.

We shall see that, from the Fifties onwards, a number of superintendents adopted liberal policies and in some cases became militant in their execution. Unlocking the doors was their main preoccupation, but it may be that the effects of this masked the persistence of more intangible forms of institutional ennui. Something which ran deep into the consciousness of hospitals was a compulsion to keep the sexes separate. Strict segregation was maintained and only occasionally, under supervised conditions, could male and female patients meet. The provision of male and female keys ensured that only their appropriate owners could enter respective male and female wards: possession of a master key, which unlocked all doors, indicated status and one-upmanship. By the 1960s, however, some hospitals were easing up on segre-gation, introducing, under the guise of social therapy, accommodation for patients who were in relationships of long standing. Sadly, the responses of many nurses to such things rarely extended beyond lasciviousness or conde-scension. In the hospital where I worked, at Hellingly, East Sussex, the small dwelling which housed two such couples was snidely referred to as 'the love nest'.

Decline

Even before Enoch Powell's speech, in-patient numbers had begun their slow but inexorable decline. Jones and Sidebotham (1962) observed how some staff saw the decline as desirable and were calling for replacement services 'in the community'. In Jones and Sidebotham's view, hospitals still had a role to play, and accelerating discharges into 'the community' might prove costly in different ways. Their gloomy outlook was motivated by the financial and structural shortages which prevailed, but they also believed that some people would always need asylum, either because 'incurably' ill or simply lacking adequate social support. Intriguingly, these writers also predicted that new services would lead to new or different forms of disability. In time, extending community psychiatric care did lead to more counselling and psychotherapy, the blossoming of a generation who appeared to be quite well but 'worried'. Arguably, this kind of provision diluted what community psychiatric services there were, such that when psychotic patients began to empty out of the closing hospitals the situation became acute, leading to angry exchanges as to the appropriate role for psychiatric personnel.

Other cautionary voices

In Kathleen Jones's (1972) opinion, hospitalisation would always be needed for some mentally ill people: she believed that growth in community services would hardly be adequate to deal with the kinds of patients traditionally managed within hospitals. In Jones's view mental hospitals were not to be feared and she thought that their dismal reputations derived from their unpopularity and not the other way around. Jokes about 'loony bins', which have their basis in fear and apprehension, tend to give rise to antagonisms towards that which is feared. These destructive processes, in her opinion, resulted in mental hospitals being seen as unworthy, whilst 'championing the new' proceeded as if being new was necessarily progressive.

Northtown Hospital

In 1962, Jones and Sidebotham inspected a range of hospitals and, in the light of their findings, surprisingly continued their support of the hospital system. Amongst their findings were refractory wards with as many as 80 patients. Although admission wards were well staffed, some had padded cells still in use. Predictably, many patients had nowhere to keep personal belongings. They also found that many patients were only allowed off their ward under nurse escort. 'There are very few discharges except by death' (Jones and Sidebotham 1962, p.60).

Also par for the course was the rigid separation of males and females. Some of the wards were truly abysmal: one had 141 patients of whom 57 were epileptic. Whilst some of these wards were now unlocked, their décor left a great deal to be desired, and whilst all of them had television sets (usually unwatched) there was precious little visible in the way of social activities.

The neurosis unit

By the mid-1960s, many hospitals had *some* wards where things looked a bit better. These were either acute admission wards or one of the growing number of neurosis units which were coming about as a result of the psychotherapeutic interests of some senior psychiatrists. More pleasant and relaxed atmospheres prevailed in neurosis units whose construction allowed for patients with less drastic diagnoses to be protected from the more depressing routines of traditional hospital fare. The one in which I worked, at Hellingly Hospital, East Sussex, was established as a separate hospital called Amberstone. Patients here were often highly conscious of *not* being patients in the main hospital. But although it had the appearance of modernity and even comparative luxury, it still adhered to a medical model of management, its one sop to alternative approaches being a registrar trained in psychoanalysis.

Other incidental findings

Male staff still slept in side rooms off some of the wards – the present writer witnessed this practice into the late 1970s. Male nurses were forbidden to enter the female nurses' accommodation and in some instances permission had to be obtained from matron to marry. It was still common to see chronic patients mechanically buffing floors to a high sheen as well as doing ward cleaning and other inside and outside domestic chores.

One finding by Jones and Sidebotham was that meetings which were called to work through some of the problems quickly fell through, except for the meeting which included patients. This meeting ended because it worked only too well: it developed an identity of its own or, as one doctor put it, 'It was at us the whole time, agitating' (Jones and Sidebotham 1962, p.76).

Metamorphosis

It had been long, if grudgingly, recognised that patients were capable of living successfully outside hospital. Community care had been talked about long enough or, to put it another way, Britain had had plenty of time to prepare for it. Where community policies were first implemented they reflected a 'hospital bias' in that they resolutely refused to look at how mental illness was conceived or how it should now be managed. For example, some purpose-built units 'in the community' continued to mimic hospital wards, and professionals continued to derive their identity through the hospital, so that the eventual closure of the hospitals must have seemed very threatening. But it was surely right that they did close, since their existence militated so strongly against any kind of civilised psychiatry. When David Cohen visited Dingleton Hospital (of Open Door fame) it was clear from the smell of urine and the sense of hopelessness that nothing had changed in years: 'Nothing worked any longer and the atmosphere was terrifying' (Cohen 1988, pp.212–213).

If anyone doubts how shabby many of these hospitals had become, they have only to read the endless government investigations into them which began to materialise from the late 1960s (see Martin 1984). Here was documented a level of abuse which went well beyond that which low staffing compliments or other deprivations might have at least helped explain. It is odd to think of these abuses as the other side of the therapeutic community coin: that whilst British psychiatry was at its communal best in some places, in others the struggle for many patients was to acquire a basic measure of dignified living.

There are many factors – which will be debated for years – as to what brought about the hospitals' downfall. What we do know is that, for the most part, they were never going to provide people with the ordinary decencies of life. It is ironic too, that it was in the hospitals that radical change would occur, albeit, as we shall see, with considerable antagonism from parent hospitals and other sources. And it is ironic, also, that many therapeutic communities, the units which most closely resemble the ethos of asylum, have survived and are even enjoying a new optimism. As for the rest, the historians will continue to pile up judgements about the purposes the asylums/hospitals served and the value that they gave (and to whom): there are unlikely to be any conclusions that will avoid giving birth to newer controversies.

References

Barton, R. (1976) *Institutional Neurosis*. Bristol: John Wright and Sons.

Bateman, J.F. and Dunham, H.W. (1948) 'The state mental hospital as a specialised community experience.' *American Journal of Psychiatry 105*, 445–458.

Belknap, I. (1956) *Human Problems of a State Mental Hospital*. New York: McGraw–Hill.

Bennet, D. (1978) 'Community psychiatry.' *British Journal of Psychiatry 132*, 209–220.

Bierer, J. (1940) 'Psychotherapy in mental hospital practice.' *Journal of Mental Science* September, 928–952.

Bion, W. (1961) *Experiences in Groups*. London: Tavistock Publications.

Bourne, H. (1953) 'The insulin myth.' *Lancet ii*, 964.

Caudill, W. (1958) *The Psychiatric Hospital as a Small Society.* Cambridge: Harvard University Press.

Clark, D. (1964) *Administrative Therapy.* London: Tavistock Publications.

Cohen, D. (1988) *Forgotten Millions.* London: Paladin.

Cohen, G.L. (1964) *What's Wrong with Hospitals?* Harmondsworth: Penguin Books.

Dicks, H.V. (1967) 'The proper study of mankind.' *British Journal of Psychiatry 113*, 1333–1344.

Dratcu, L. (2000) 'Antipsychotic formulations.' *Community Mental Health 2*, 4, 10–14.

Foucault, M. (1971) *Madness and Civilisation: A History of Insanity in the Age of Reason.* London: Tavistock Publications.

Goffman, E. (1961) *Asylums.* Harmondsworth: Penguin Books.

Hawker, R. (1985) 'Gatekeeping: a traditional and contemporary function of the nurse.' In R. White (ed) *Political Issues in Nursing: Past, Present and Future.* London: John Wiley and Sons.

Hawkins, T.R. and Tibbetts, R.W. (1956) 'Intravenous acetylcholine therapy in neurosis.' *The Journal of Mental Science 102*, 426 [390 new series] 43–51.

Hinshelwood, R.D. (1983) 'Editorial: our three-way see-saw.' *International Journal of Therapeutic Communities 4*, 167–168.

Jones, K. (1972) *A History of the Mental Health Services.* London: Routledge and Kegan Paul.

Jones, K. and Sidebotham, R. (1962) *Mental Hospitals At Work.* London: Routledge and Kegan Paul.

Jones, M. (1952) *Social Psychiatry.* Harmondsworth: Penguin Books.

Martin, D.V. (1955) 'Institutionalisation.' *Lancet* (3 December), 1188–1190.

Martin, J.P. (1984) *Hospitals in Trouble.* Oxford: Blackwell.

Nightingale, F. (1860) [1952] *Notes on Nursing.* London: Duckworth.

Porter, R. (1990) *Mind-forg'd Manacles.* Harmondsworth: Penguin.

Powell, E. (1961) *Report of the Annual Conference of the National Association for Mental Health.* London: National Association for Mental Health.

Rees, T. P. (1957) 'Back to moral treatment and community care.' *Journal of Mental Science 103*, 303–313.

Scull, A. (1979) *Museums of Madness.* London: Allen Lane.

Stanton, A.H. and Schwartz, M.S. (1954) *The Mental Hospital.* New York: Basic Books.

Whiteley, S. (1979) 'Progress and reflection.' In R.D. Hinshelwood and N. Manning (eds) *Therapeutic Communities: Reflections and Progress.* London: Routledge and Kegan Paul.

Wing, J.K. (1970) *Institutionalism and Schizophrenia: A Comparative Study of Three Mental Hospitals.* London: Cambridge University Press.

World Health Organisation (1953) *Expert Committee on Mental Health 3rd Report.* Geneva: WHO.

CHAPTER 3

Joshua Bierer: Striving For Power

I am a grateful pupil of Adler.

Bierer (1940)

Joshua Bierer was born in Austria in 1901. He obtained an MD in Vienna in 1928 and then trained in Adlerian psychology. His training analysis (1927–1928) was with Dr A. Neuer who, together with Alfred Adler, was to be the dominant influence on his professional life. As Dicks observed, 'Bierer was still applying his strictly held Adlerian concepts years later at the Marlborough Day Hospital' (Dicks 1970, p.182).

Unlike Freud, Adler placed great importance on the idea of individuals having a purpose in life – in many ways Adler pre-empted the much later American self psychology of Abraham Maslow (1987) and Carl Rogers (1978) – but he also stressed the need to view human behaviour within social settings. According to Bierer, 'Adler advocated a more active role for the psychotherapist. He originated the science of the family' (Bierer 1951, p.47). It was this combination of individual and social psychology which had a direct bearing on Bierer establishing Britain's first day hospital, the Marlborough, which he saw as providing 'a distinct atmosphere combining various forms of individual and group psychotherapy, rehabilitation and resocialisation' (Bierer 1951, p.54).

More Biererian than Adlerian

The problem was that, like his mentor Adler, Bierer tended to overcompensate, in the eyes of many becoming far too eager to define his work as seminal and weighty. In effect: 'I invented British social psychiatry. I set up the first community day hospital. I can do everything. I can run everything.'

He claimed to be both Zionist and Socialist. Like many others, with the rise of Nazism he came to England and was the first psychotherapist appointed to a post in a public hospital (at Runwell). Appointed in 1935, the first medical superintendent at Runwell, Dr Rolf Strom-Olsen, had surrounded himself with quite young, bright people – for instance, a start was made on what was (erroneously) believed to be a promising area of psychiatric research, namely electroencephalography (EEG) under Dr S. J. Last – and the hospital acquired an international reputation in this respect. Proud of his 'showpiece' hospital, Strom-Olsen had also established outpatient departments in nearby general hospitals but his most far-reaching departure was Bierer's inaugural appointment to the post of psychotherapist. Runwell was the first planned mental hospital in Britain since the First World War and although it had over a thousand patients when it opened in 1937 it was still 'the best appointed mental hospital in the country' and the only English hospital comprising small self-contained units whose purpose, according to Jefferies and Lee (1986), was to combat institutionalisation.

As a member of the Royal Army Medical Corps Bierer was, for a while, associated with the experiments taking place at the Northfield Military Neurosis Centre where he had established group psychotherapy in his own ward and in his own style. Harrison (2000) records that Northfield participants remember him as 'being on the sidelines' and the other Northfield psychiatrists considered him something of a lightweight. An early indication of eccentricity, whilst at Northfield, is that he had his wife sing opera to the residents, presumably as some kind of enlightenment.

Through the Institute of Social Psychiatry and the British Association of Social Psychiatry, both of which he founded, he pushed forward community facilities for patients with long-standing and severe psychiatric disabilities. In this respect, he was a dedicated clinician. That said, the organisations which he founded, despite impressive sounding names, were merely vehicles by which he could expound his views. And yet the *International Journal of Social Psychiatry* which he established in 1955, and edited, continues to publish articles to the high standard that he set. Also, his community-based facilities were innovative and precedent setting.

Bierer was an enthusiastic lecturer both in Britain and abroad and wrote extensively on social psychiatry and rehabilitation: in his *British Medical Journal* obituary (1985) it was recalled that 'he had many firsts to his credit'. Yet almost all the key figures of the '1950s reform movements' in British psychiatry ignore him completely; he is rarely mentioned in any of their texts and is today practically forgotten.

Early days

In 1940, Dr Bierer delivered to a meeting of the Royal Medico-Psychological Association his beliefs regarding the practice of psychotherapy in mental hospitals. He had perceived that behind the hypodermic syringe lay deeper, unconscious, motivations which governed relationships with patients but which were largely inaccessible. Further, he charged that – in relation to most psychiatric problems – some modification of the environment is necessary if effective therapy is to take place. To this end he set up, in 1940 at Runwell, a Patients' Social Club, reasoning that this would help its members become more socially active and responsible: it would also encourage more flexible relationships between the sexes. The club was intended to be autonomous, with each member casting a vote for chairman, secretary, committee and sub-committees for a variety of interests and pursuits. It met three times weekly (for sport, entertainment and intellectual work) and a bi-monthly magazine was published – only articles from patients accepted. Initially, Bierer proposed to keep staff out but this was objected to and medical and other staff did eventually participate in the club's affairs. Visiting Runwell in the early Sixties, Gerda Cohen asked him if these experiments had succeeded:

> Succeed? What does that really mean? One schizophrenic used to lie all day in bed. One couple got married – yes, we dared to mix men and women – you saw them at the club holding hands. (Cohen 1964, p.174)

These innovations in recreational self-management by patients have been largely neglected in the literature and only one recent chronicler of therapeutic communities (Harrison 2000) has seen fit to credit Bierer, citing his patient/social clubs as a precursor to similar schemes begun at Northfield.

Community treatment programmes

Bierer also devised a community treatment programme comprising twice weekly meetings of up to 50 patients of whom about one third usually took part. These sessions aimed to dampen tensions amongst patients as well as counteract any anti-social feelings potentially present. Bierer found the meetings difficult – patients can and do argue! – and he worried about them going in 'the wrong direction', although he never said what he meant by this. He seems not to have appreciated the possibility of people correcting each other's asocial behaviours within a therapeutic milieu and it remains an open question whether, as in Harrison's (2000) view, this work was a kind of dry run for more radical departures later on. Bierer's work was a practical step in this direction but it was conceptually fragile, and it is this that ultimately wrecks his ambition. His efforts to influence British psychiatry were not much more than exhortation and he failed to provide persuasive rationales for much of what he did; we are rarely told *why* something is beneficial and are generally left in the dark as to how the changes he proposed could be more widely implemented. Partly also, his failure to appreciate British distrust of political stridency antagonised a more cautious, conservative audience and, as the 1950s approached, medical colleagues began to tire of his assertions and declarations: although their finding him tiresome may have had less to do with critiquing his ideas – the tendency has been to dismiss rather than engage with him – and more to do with a rejection due to embarrassment at his lack of social graces.

Teamwork

Bierer took particular interest in the role that occupational therapists could play in rehabilitation. He insisted that information from different sources should be shared with them so to enhance patient care. He boosted their status, arguing that therapeutic work should never be hobby-oriented or humdrum, advocating work that would be meaningful as well as consistent with the interests and backgrounds of the patients involved. In fact, occupational therapists fulfilled a therapeutic need in day hospitals and therapeutic communities generally. It may be recalled that Maxwell Jones was never fully comfortable working with nurses (Clark 1994) whom he probably saw as representing medical concepts of treatment and intolerant of the loose-structured regimes which characterised the therapeutic community. Whilst a small number of nurses were psychoanalytically trained or congenial to therapeutic community principles, most were certainly not and many (see Chapter 4) were actually opposed to change within hospitals. At the time occupational therapists were more articulate and more congenial towards working within non-traditional milieus. An alternative view is that Bierer favoured occupational therapists because he would have found it difficult to impose his views on senior and/or entrenched nurses and their hierarchical management systems.

Addressing the congregation

Bierer's address to the Royal Medico-Psychological Association in 1940 was received with politeness. His request for a viable psychotherapy practice within the mental hospitals met with dismay, largely, it seems, on economic and not medical grounds. Many senior psychiatrists of the day were medical superintendents with wide-ranging financial and administrative responsibilities. Individual psychotherapy was (and is) time-consuming of therapeutic man-hours and know-how (Clark 1956). Indeed, the development of group therapies within therapeutic communities may partly reflect the absence of people competent to practise individual therapy (Martin *et al.* 1954), as well as the economic advantages of group approaches.

Although, by 1940, the military had not yet conscripted many doctors, travel had become difficult and attending conferences was not easy. Present at Bierer's address was Maxwell Jones's great friend, T. P. Rees, physician superintendent of Warlingham Park Hospital and a significant psychiatrist at this time. It was Rees's contention that hospitals should be places of personal growth and not custodians of personality failure. Rees later became a member of the Royal Commission on Mental Illness and Mental Deficiency (1954–1957) which presaged the 1959 Mental Health Act. Earlier, he had part authored the World Health Organisation's influential Third Report (1953). Both innovative and pragmatic, Rees asked Bierer if hospital-based psychotherapists should possess medical degrees: would it not be possible, he said, to staff a hospital with lay psychotherapists under the direction of a psychiatrist? Although given time to respond, Bierer ignored the question, perhaps indicating his aversion for the 'non-medical man' holding psychiatric authority. For his part, Rees (1954, 1956, 1957) never mentioned Bierer in his own work, not even negatively.

The Sunny Side Club

According to Bierer and Haldane (1941), any patient could be a committee member and membership was retained after discharge. In addition, members of staff needed an invitation from a patient to attend meetings, most of which were about organising and implementing recreational events. Fortnightly discussions of a personal nature did take place but 'in a general way'. Bierer stated that problems could not be solved without mixing with and learning to treat others appropriately within a community: attitudes can only be changed through interaction – and are poorly affected by theory. Unlike the therapeutic community practitioners, however, he did not regard the hospital community as in any way coterminous with society at large: he lacked conceptual understanding of what a therapeutic community might mean, how it might contain and define the confusion or threat that accompanies change. We have also to consider his ambivalence towards the idea of 'unrestrained' patients, understandable enough as this was at the time. In 1884 Daniel Hack Tuke stated, 'It is easy to talk glibly about the liberty of the subject, and so difficult to guard against the licence into which that too often degenerates' (in Jones 1972, p.170).

Such views were common in Britain in the late Forties and Fifties as the doors of the asylums were being unlocked. Whilst Bierer protested that it was 'regulations' which prevented his patients from taking complete control of the club, he insisted that a member of staff always be present at meetings. Insisting that the patients were autonomous for the club part of their hospital lives, he still believed that staff should influence and advise and he always worried about things 'going wrong', typically fretting when an 'intelligent' patient organised a quiz that proved too much for less able patients. In fairness, the question of the club's autonomy was recognised and Bierer seems to have taken part as a kind of revered guest rather than its ruler.

Yet he was always at odds with the more democratic hospital leaders who followed him; Foulkes (1964) refers to his leader-centred and more active methods, and comparing him to Maxwell Jones, said that they differed considerably in their attitudes. In this, Foulkes appears to be referring to group-work particularly and the distinctions to be made between the analytic (Bierer) and non-analytic (Jones) approaches. More generally, there was little sense of Bierer's social clubs operating within a leaderless milieu, or of them critically influencing traditional hierarchical systems. On the other hand, his town-based community centres were seminal in the provision of community psychiatry. The problem is that, at the time, community psychiatry was a miscellaneous, stop/go affair with attention continuing to be paid to the achievements of hospital psychiatry. As such, it is not surprising that Bierer's only credit in psychiatric history is for his hospital clubs, what Ivor Browne (1994) calls 'probably the least of his achievements'. What seems overdue is a more careful assessment of his community-based programmes, and their function as prototypes for later developments.

Inspirational

In 1940 Bierer's work had few precedents. He could draw upon psychoanalysis, of course, even if it afforded him little in the way of practical help; actually, differences between the pragmatic psychiatric pioneers and psychoanalysts were particularly marked during the Thirties and early Forties – the heyday of psychoanalysis in Britain – and psychoanalysis found little favour with either the open door 'movement' or rehabilitation psychiatry generally.

H.V. Dicks, a Tavistock man, recalled being told by T. P. Rees: 'You Tavi boys had a great chance after the War and you did not take it' (Dicks 1970, p.183). Dicks was inclined to agree, commenting upon the analytic reserve and exclusiveness of the Tavistock in relation to changes in psychiatry then taking place. Although hospital-based, these changes were socially oriented – Jones's work at the Belmont for instance – and reflected a bias against the focus of Main (1946) and Bion (1961) where the therapist played a central, interpretative role and which led to the kinds of work which characterised the Cassel Hospital and Ingrebourne Centre. Bierer was too idiosyncratic for psychoanalysis (ditto R.D. Laing) and his work at the Marlborough took on a more hybrid and extemporaneous quality. This was partly due to his laudable willingness to accept all comers as patients even if this hindered the development of coherent strategies of care. Developing consistent patterns of care was also made more difficult by the increasing pace of discharges which diminished opportunities for patient sociability. In a recent retrospective, Clarke (1999) took the view that this constant fall off in sociable patients (into community care) induced a malaise into what had been a thriving institutional psychiatry.

The Marlborough Day Hospital

From 1941, Bierer began to see his social clubs as the foundation for therapeutic day centres that would extend into the community. Such centres appear to have existed in some form in both the Soviet Union and Canada, but this was their first outing in Britain. Accordingly, he initiated the day hospital movement by setting up a Social Psychotherapy Centre at Hampstead in 1946, which became known as the Marlborough in 1954. It was set in what had been Thomas Henry Huxley's house and Bierer converted the mews and garage at the back into a night hospital. According to Ivor Browne, Bierer 'had a day and night hospital by the time I got there but it was closed at the weekend' (Healy 1992, p.6). This development allowed Bierer to pursue his 'philosophy' of providing sociotherapeutic centres which would be geographically and administratively distant from their parent hospital, as well as being relatively free from institutional pressures. Typically, he announced his intention of 'abolishing the mental hospital', but he can hardly have imagined that his day centres would have been an adequate alternative. As interested in style as in substance (Sim 1994), he naturally approached the Royal Family to open the Hampstead centre but it appears that Princess Margaret declined.

The actual term 'day hospital' was first used by Cameron (1958) in the USA but was appropriated by Bierer shortly after. It quickly became a synonym for many types of unit operating at different degrees of attachment to parent hospitals. Bierer (1951) suggested that the term be restricted to the independent and detached unit which characterised his Hampstead centre. However, the detached unit was not a popular option and of the 38 'day hospitals' visited by Farndale (1961) in the late Fifties, only two fitted Bierer's criteria.

At the Marlborough, patients attended from one to 12 or more times per week. All forms of treatments were available, although Bierer emphasised group therapies. Attempts were made to help all patients regardless of diagnosis or severity of illness or disturbance. There was a children's service and a 12-bedded emergency unit for those facing short-term crises. A warm social atmosphere prevailed, with what Patmore (1985) calls 'a lack of attention to professional boundaries'. In this, Patmore is not referring to a 'flattening' of roles between staff and patients, but rather a matrix of relationships bordering on nonchalance and easy-going atmospherics. Kennard (1983) states that the place developed into a sophisticated therapeutic community using a variety of group methods and involving patients in its administration. But when Clark (1994) visited it in the 1960s, he found little to support its social or therapeutic claims, and Hinshelwood (1980), who worked there, describes a confused and conflict-ridden environment. Professor Kathleen Jones (1972) called day hospitals 'the panacea' of the Fifties, and points out that many of them did not survive. As Farndale (1961) notes, they were subject to geographic and demographic problems in addition to problems of role and direction. The Marlborough closed in 1978 from a combination of staff difficulties and external pressures. Kennard (1983) states that its closure 'afforded occasion for much reflection on the difficulties experienced there in the last few years': see also Foster (1979), Grunberg (1979) and *especially* Baron (1987).

Full of humility

Although the Marlborough was not a community day centre of the kind that we now think as such, it was nevertheless a serious departure from traditional psychiatry. Bierer had told Farndale that mental illness was partly a function of social attitudes, and that his unit was about educating the public as much as anything. Started as a unit in its own right, the declared intention was to 'replace the mental hospital' and not just supplement it. And, in the view of some, it was successful: Professor Ivor Browne (1994) spent a year there in the late Fifties and recalls startling reductions in hospital re-admissions for people who were its patients. Browne's progressive, social psychiatry was influenced by the Marlborough, and he sees Bierer as a true pioneer. Myre Sim likewise contends that Bierer's work merits a higher regard than it has received; he states that Bierer *did* provide interesting ideas to underscore his work. Certainly he made a good job of editing his journal: papers were carefully scrutinised and helpful comments were frequently provided by him for authors.

In a review of therapeutic group analysis, Foulkes pays tribute to many whose names figure prominently in the history of therapeutic communities but says that, 'Above all, credit is due to Joshua Bierer and his pioneer work which he started before the war at Runwell Hospital' (Foulkes 1964, p.216). Others remember Bierer as someone who told a 'tall tale', who exuded paternal benevolence, a stance curiously at odds with the democratic systems of care which he publicly espoused.

Hinshelwood (1980) says that direction is most apparent when embodied in a charismatic leader and that the Marlborough was dominated by Bierer. But, of course, every therapeutic community had its charismatic father figure and each was to suffer (sometimes catastrophically) upon his departure unless and until replaced by another. This is the central dilemma of therapeutic communities, and in Bierer's case a great deal more charm was involved than most. Forever claiming that he had founded social psychiatry, the magnitude of the claim was the measure of its meaninglessness. His achievements were noteworthy, true, but a theory of social psychiatry had existed at least since Durkheim's *Suicide*. Mayer-Gross, Slater and Roth (1969) noted that Adolph Meyer had implemented training programmes for psychiatric social workers as far back as 1918 and they go on to say that 'the importance of social factors in psychiatric illness had been recognised long before' (Mayer-Gross *et al.* 1969, p.7).

All comers

Bierer consistently demonstrated strong feelings for the more disadvantaged types. Patmore (1985) notes his particular commitment to the psychotic patient, and the *British Medical Journal* (1985) observed that he had been 'full of humanity, he fought for all those who were deprived and underprivileged' (Patmore 1985, p.163). His treatment programmes encompassed all forms of mental disturbance. Diagnosis, he said, was of little relevance and he claimed to make little use of it: it did not help him in his work; it did not relate to prognosis; it could even prove harmful since 'it leads to a certain satisfaction in the mind of the doctor'. He argued that it accentuates rather than minimises symptoms which in turn provoke other symptoms. From a psychotherapeutic standpoint, it's clear that he was placing diagnoses within what he saw as the 'organic period' in psychiatry: that epoch was now past and *he*, Joshua Bierer, was ushering in a new period of social/psychological psychiatry in keeping with *his* discoveries about the true (societal) nature of mental illness.

Although mainly preoccupied with rehabilitating people with chronic disabilities, he believed that psychotherapy was suitable for such patients, that it:

> Could be applied to a wide range of conditions including schizophrenia, just as much as depression or the neuroses. He had an amazing facility to break through to people – into someone who was mute. Once started he would be quite liable to keep them talking all afternoon. He could be psychopathic too – drifting off into something else, leaving them high, and dry. (Healy 1992, p.7)

Unsung heroes: the limits of literature

Bierer is hardly mentioned in the social psychiatric literature except by Foulkes and, of course, Foulkes was a friend – he came from the same part of the world and could even be said to have discovered Bierer. Foulkes admired bravery and the intrepid Bierer could always be counted on for that. As I've said, there are some references in the literature in relation to his day hospitals, particularly the setting up of the Marlborough, as well as, most recently, a short summary of his time at Northfield after the Second World War (Harrison 2000), but other than that, he is barely mentioned.

Is it possible that he set up too much? It's difficult to say, since we cannot trust the accuracy of his accounts. He claimed, truthfully according to David Clark (1994), to have established two of the first kibbutzim in the 1920s. He also laid claim to research of an 'earth-shaking variety which mysteriously went astray in the back seat of a London taxi'. His grandfather was Court Physician to the King of Serbia (a possible). He gave himself a distinguished war record, dubiously. And, of course, he was brash in presenting his work which shows in his writing, which is declarative and rarely instructive.

Perhaps it is the *writers* who get remembered? It is noteworthy that psychiatric 'best sellers' such as *Asylums* or *The Divided Self* were really well written. Bierer, of course, wrote badly and, as well, 'spoke poorly' with an accent that was sometimes difficult to penetrate, the latter a quality he also shared with S.H. Foulkes (see Harrison 2000, p.55). With his 'foreign' medical credentials he may have cut an outlandish figure in an 'establishment' context of British medicine. For example, in the contest which took place for the Presidency of the Association of Social Psychiatry, what were the factors which led to the appointment of Morris Carstair and not Bierer? The former held the Chair in Psychiatry at Edinburgh University, had a good record with the Medical Research Council, was the son of missionaries to India, a darling of the Left and had impeccable academic credentials. In retrospect, it would have been surprising had Bierer been given the post although with his entrepreneurial skills, he would probably have done a good job!

Bierer was 50 years old by the time the Second World War ended; much older than contemporaries like Main, Jones and Bion, who would become legends in British psychiatry. Also, he retired earlier than them, fading over the years and so not seeming to be a part of the liberalism of the 1950s which he represented. His poor literary skills do not completely account for his diminished reputation, since only a few of his contemporaries wrote pleasantly and some hardly at all. Yet they might still present conceptually interesting papers and, as mentioned, Bierer's writing proclaims a lot but is weak on ideas. Having said that, the Fifties was an era which rated practical achievement highly. Maxwell Jones at one point describes himself as an 'action agent', and Bierer was certainly active. So was it the quality of his work that was suspect? Recall Clark's visit to the Marlborough in the Sixties, a visit which left him distinctly unimpressed. Yet no one acquired more 'firsts' than Bierer and a single judgement on one of his projects hardly explains why he was so neglected. So why the virtual disappearance from psychiatric history?

A bit of a charmer

To begin with, Bierer was hard to ignore at the best of times: a flamboyant middle European, who tirelessly organised conferences that could (and often did) degenerate into truculent, messy affairs – on one occasion Maxwell Jones became very angry with his overbearing and petulant meddling. Often 'puckish and grandiose', many people came to distrust him. He could charm money out of the trees, yet he was benevolent and his wife claimed, with some truth, that they had nothing. A refugee, he had some of the insecurity which such experience produces and which may have had something to do with his desire for attention.

He was quite good-looking, taking on a venerable look later in life, and was regarded by many, at the time, as something of a 'ladies' man': not the view of his *British Medical Journal* obituary (1985), which describes him as 'a devoted family man'. Both versions are actually true in so far as he had several wives and families. Such was the sexual hypocrisy of the times it is difficult to work out a true picture, but one description that has 'the great man' falling into a swoon with acolyte lady social workers frantically running about exclaiming, 'The doctor! The doctor! Something has happened to the doctor!', probably reflects a truer 'sexual' picture.

At the Marlborough he dominated (Hinshelwood 1980), opulently wandering about: some rumours have him distributing sodium amytal capsules to all and sundry and although potentially malicious, some of his contemporaries say that 'this picture fits'. A 'man of abundant charm and charismatic personality', he could also at times '…appear brusque and difficult'. Once called 'A Moses always looking for Israelites', he appears to have had the affection of his patients who were devoted to him. Not eccentric, but clearly larger than life, there was much 'rascality' in him, although he was not a rascal, and emphatically not a charlatan. He had something of the flavour of an 'eastern European brigand': yet his buccaneering spirit could hardly cause offence, for others had this quality too. Thomas Percy Rees, superintendent at Warlingham Park, for one, who succeeded by force of personality, the capacity to inspire. Bierer, however, left few disciples, his inclination to quarrel tending to fend off would-be followers or admirers.

Strengths and weaknesses

In many ways, Bierer's career epitomises both the strengths and weaknesses of the period. The advent of the medical superintendents went hand in hand with a growth in medicalisation (and overcrowding) of patients' lives. Bierer (never a superintendent) always seemed averse to drug treatments – although he used them – preferring community care or unorthodox drug approaches such as LSD (where he may have had some success). He ventured outside the 'the asylum' when others, Maxwell Jones for instance, seemed content to be a revolutionary on the *inside*. Yet it is regrettable that much of what Bierer attempted was haphazard, unanalysed, and often coloured by vanity. The times favoured trial and error and new and different forms of therapy, and lacked the eyebrow-raising responses that would accompany such experiments today. Bierer personifies the worst of this kind of ill-thought-out and speculative approach, whilst in some ways symbolising the best, which was often quite inventive therapeutic social psychiatry. Opinions divided: on a fact-finding tour of hospitals in the Sixties, journalist Gerda Cohen was informed by one superintendent that Dr Bierer was 'a charlatan whilst another pronounced him a near genius' (Cohen 1964, p.173).

No doubt opinion would divide as equally today, although the majority view now is that flamboyant, radical psychiatry ran out of steam by the end of the Sixties. Discussing his arrival in England and his first brushes with orthodox, hierarchical psychiatry, Bierer told Cohen:

> I found a double set of prisoners – patient and nurse, each locked in her own cell. The matron did not take meals with her Deputy. How I did miss Vienna... (Cohen 1964, p.173)

But he had arrived at a time when British psychiatry was ready to embark on its most effervescent period: at a time when there would soon be no shortage of charismatic practitioners and innovative movements. Bierer was the most seductive of all, but, regrettably, his better work wilted in the heat of his belligerent immodesty. But he was a victim too: caught up in a conservative medical establishment which responded to him with snobbery and some disdain, he was unable to articulate his way out of this or form the kinds of fellowships which might have helped him out.

References

Baron, C. (1987) *Asylum into Anarchy*. London: Free Association Books.

Bierer, J. (1940) 'Therapy in mental hospital practice.' *Journal of Mental Science* 928–52.

Bierer, J. (1951) *The Day Hospital: An Experiment in Social Psychiatry and Synthoanalytic Psychotherapy*. London: H.K. Lewis and Co. Ltd.

Bierer, J. and Haldane, F.P. (1941) 'A self-governed patients' social club in a public mental hospital.' *Journal of Mental Science* 419–426.

Bion, W. (1961) *Experiences in Groups*. London: Tavistock Publications.

Boag, T.J. (1960) 'Further developments in the day hospital.' *American Journal of Psychiatry 116* (March), 801–806.

Bowen, A. (1993) Personal correspondence.

British Medical Journal (1985) 'Obituary: Joshua Bierer.' 290 (12 January), 163.

Browne, I. (1994) Personal correspondence.

Cameron, D.E. (1958) 'Proceedings of the 1958 Day Hospital Conference.' American Psychiatric Association.

Cawley, R.H. (1992) 'Bierer's precepts today and tomorrow.' *International Journal of Social Psychiatry 38*, 87–94.

Clark, D. (1956) 'Functions of the mental hospital.' *Lancet* (17 November), 1005–9.

Clark, D. (1994) Personal correspondence.

Clarke, L. (1993) 'The opening of doors in British mental hospitals in the 1950s.' *History of Psychiatry 4*, 527–51.

Clarke, L. (1999) *Challenging Ideas in Psychiatric Nursing*. London: Routledge.

Cohen, G.L. (1964) *What's Wrong with Hospitals?* Harmondsworth: Penguin Books.

Davis, B. (1981) 'Social skills in nursing.' In M. Argyle (ed) *Social Skills and Health*. London: Methuen.

Dicks, H.V. (1970) *50 Years of the Tavistock Clinic*. London: Routledge and Kegan Paul.

Farndale, J. (1961) *The Day Hospital Movement in Great Britain*. Oxford: Pergamon Press.

Foster, A. (1979) 'The collapse of the Marlborough Day Community.' Paper presented at the 2nd Windsor Conference: Anglo-Dutch Workshop on Therapeutic Communities. Windsor.

Foulkes, S.H. (1964) *Group Analysis*. London: George Allen and Unwin Ltd.

Foulkes, S.H. (1975) *Group-analytic Psychotherapy: An Interface Book*. London: Gordon and Breech Science Publishers Ltd.

Grunberg, S.R. (1979) 'The implications of the erosion of authority in a therapeutic community.' Paper presented at the 2nd Windsor Conference: Anglo-Dutch Workshop on Therapeutic Communities. Windsor.

Harrison, T. (2000) *Bion, Rickman, Foulkes and the Northfield Experiments*. London: Jessica Kingsley Publishers.

Healy, D. (1992) Interview: 'In conversation with Ivor Browne.' *Psychiatric Bulletin 16*, 1–9.

Hinshelwood, R. (1980) 'Ale seeds of disaster.' *International Journal of Therapeutic Communities 1*, 3, 181–188.

Jefferies, M. and Lee, J.A. (1986) *The Hospitals of Southend*. Chichester: Phillimore and Co. Ltd.

Jones, K. (1972) *A History of the Mental Health Services*. London: Routledge and Kegan Paul.

Kennard, D. (1983) *An Introduction to Therapeutic Communities*. London: Routledge and Kegan Paul.

Main, T. (1946) 'The hospital as a therapeutic community.' *Bulletin of the Menninger Clinic 10*, 66–70.

Martin, D., Glatt, M. and Weeks, K.F. (1954) 'An experimental unit for the community treatment of neurosis.' *Journal of Mental Science* (October), 983–989.

Maslow, A. (1987) *Motivation and Personality*. London: Harper and Row.

Mayer-Gross, W., Slater, E. and Roth, M. (1969) *Clinical Psychiatry*, 3rd edn. London: Bailliere Tindall.

Patmore, C. (1985) 'News section: mental health pioneer.' *Openmind 13* (February/ March).

Pitt, B. and Markowe, M. (1963) 'A new pattern in day hospital development: the West Middlesex Hospital.' *British Journal of Psychiatry 109*, 29–36.

Ramon, S. (1985) *Psychiatry in Britain, Meaning and Policy*. London: Croom Helm.

Rees, T.P. (1954) 'The unlocked door.' *Lancet* (6 November), 953.

Rees, T.P. (1956) 'Statement to the Annual Meeting of the RMPA.' *International Journal of Social Psychiatry 2*, 152.

Rees, T.P. (1957) 'Back to moral treatment and community care.' *Journal of Mental Science 103*, 431, 303–313.

Rogers, C. (1978) *Carl Rogers on Personal Power*. London: Constable.

Sim, M. (1994) Personal correspondence.

Vaughn, P.J. (1961) 'Developments in psychiatric day care.' *British Journal of Psychiatry 147*, 1–4.

White, R. (1985) 'Political regulators in British nursing.' In R. White (ed) *Political Issues in Nursing*, Vol. 1. Chichester: John Wiley.

World Health Organisation (1953) *Third Report of the Expert Committee on Mental Health: Technical Report Series no. 73*. Geneva: WHO Hospital.

CHAPTER 4

Unlocking the Doors in the 1950s

I know the grass beyond the door,
The sweet keen smell.

Dante Gabriel Rossetti (1863)

Introduction

This chapter is about unlocking doors in British mental hospitals during the 1950s. It makes the point that change resulted from the activities of a small number of enthusiastic medical superintendents and despite sustained opposition from psychiatric nurses. Although the discussion involves only a limited number of hospitals, this is because only a small number of open door activists publicised their activities. Whilst many British hospitals engaged in open door activities they did so selectively, tentatively and sometimes furtively. Of course, the 'open door movement' (as it came to be known) represents only the more visible aspects of change and may have overshadowed other developments such as the radical departures of emerging therapeutic communities. The open door adventure was an interesting barometer of change nevertheless; therapeutic communities were hardly representative of hospital practice overall whereas unlocking hospital doors became fairly widespread.

The push to open the doors stemmed from pragmatic concerns about the everyday welfare of patients. There was little theorising, so that events were less motivated by discussions about social therapies, for instance, and more by an awareness of how awful asylum life had become for its inmates. This was evident in Thomas Rees's (1957) Presidential Address to the British Psychiatric Association when he called for a return to the Moral Treatment of the 19th century, which he saw as the principled basis for more liberal programmes of psychiatric care. However, Rees's description of the period between the 19th century and the 1950s as one of unrelieved custodial gloom is not entirely accurate. Lenzie Asylum had all of its doors open in 1881 and ten years later, when Burdett conducted a national survey, open doors were in part use in 13 English County Borough asylums. Later, under Dr Saxty Good, Littlemore Hospital in Oxford appears to have been the first mental hospital to open its doors in the 20th century – in 1922 – and had indeed unlocked more than half its doors by about 1935. However, these were isolated cases and progress from then on was slow.

Different opinions

The post-war era favoured change and fewer walks of life needed it more than the moribund mental hospitals. Entering Fulbourn Hospital in 1953 was, said David Clark, 'like cycling back into the nineteenth century. The NHS and the twentieth century made hardly an impression on the place' (Barraclough 1986, p.43). Clark's account of how he set about changing things – retold in Barraclough 1986 – is vivid, entertaining and enlightening. Clark's own achievement bears out my contention that it was the hospital superintendents who brought about change. Although little evidence supports an open door *movement* amongst the superintendents, a movement of sorts occurred in respect of the small number of hospitals which threw open their doors completely. According to David Clark (1975), however, liberal policies are better reflected in the 90 per cent of patients living in open wards throughout the system overall, rather than in the small number of radically reformed hospitals. But it was the *trumpeting* of the latter, the 'Open Sesame' decrees, which defined the period as one of progressive promise. However, in addition to robust superintendents, more complicated, psycho-social factors impinged on the effectiveness of changes underway. Unlocking the doors was an act whose execution depended on little more than an expression of executive power: that was the straightforward part. Creating and sustaining contexts within which innovation would flourish was something different.

Some background notes

By the early years of the last century the hospitals had become bigger, individuality had lost out to routine and nursing *en masse* became a necessity. The Great War (1914–1918) exacerbated conditions with many staff going to the services, their places being taken by less experienced people. This combination of staff shortages and inexperience, coupled with recession-fuelled cut-backs, made custodialism much worse. Hunter and Macalpine (1974) record that 2000 (or 90 per cent) of the patients at Friern Hospital lived under lock and key during the Twenties and Thirties, as against 75 per cent about 20 years earlier.

By the 1930s, however, improvements were taking place. Staffing levels were improving due to increased unemployment 'freeing up' labour markets.

In addition, legislative and administrative changes – the setting up of a Ministry of Health in 1919 and a Nurses' Registration Act in the same year – were starting to have measured, positive effects.

The 1930 Mental Treatment Act provided for voluntary hospital admissions as well as the setting up of out-patient psychiatric clinics. Progress following the act was slow, however, with only 35 per cent voluntary admissions nationally occurring by 1938 (Jones 1960). Even this figure disguises wide variations in the country as a whole and, for instance, at Friern Hospital, only 35 out of 2035 patients had been reclassified as voluntary as late as 1945.

Nevertheless, the 1930 Act facilitated early diagnoses and treatment of reversible conditions: previously, hospitals had ignored all but the severely disabled. For those already hospitalised, however, changes in legal status (as was the case following the 1959 Act) were often paper exercises: there is no evidence of anyone informing patients about the practical implications of their altered status. Bickford – always a sceptic – identified many patients, now re-classified as 'voluntary', as 'chronic schizophrenics who have little idea of where they are or what they are doing, and have no more understanding of their new status than of their old' (Bickford 1958, p.423).

Much later, Gostin (1977, p.16) also noted the ironies surrounding the 1959 legislation and its provision of informal status. Who, asked Gostin, can be sure what transpires in the living rooms of distressed people on the issue of whether they should or should not be admitted into hospital. How certain can we be that they have not been subject to undue pressure from family or professionals to comply with their hospital admission?

The hospitals had a bad war

During the Second World War, psychiatric beds were commandeered for general medical services. Hunter and Macalpine (1974) describe 215 male and 409 female beds being given over for this purpose at Friern Hospital, with incumbent patients being sent to other wards and hospitals. On the male side overcrowding was 20 per cent, and 14 per cent on the female. As with the Great War, existing privations were made worse by reduced staffing levels due to nurses entering military service. By now the overcrowding had led to truly deplorable conditions. Dr David Rice, Superintendent of Hellingly Hospital, East Sussex, described dormitories so overcrowded that the patients had to climb into their beds from the bottom, there being no spaces between them: each patient had a chamber pot; windows were shut to prevent patients 'catching a chill'; gleaming floors were layered with repeated applications of

Johnson's wax and; to top it all, open fires added to the unmistakable odour brought on by the combination of all of these and called by Dr Rice 'the asylum smell'.

Overcrowding continued into the 1950s, both in locked and unlocked systems. Whilst one might have anticipated that open door systems would have led to increased discharges of patients, the open door often meant a *reluctance* to discharge, because it was feared that freed up beds would lead to 'undesirable patients' being transferred into them. But, in general, opinion in the 1950s favoured change and whilst resistance by the nurses and some doctors impeded things, medical superintendents were now publicly castigating institutionalisation as *the* major problem and calling for policies to combat it.

The hospitals concerned

Dingleton Hospital, Melrose, led the way and was completely open by October 1949 following a three-year transition during which wards were progressively unlocked (Ratcliff 1962). Mapperley Hospital, Nottingham – where only one ward was open in 1931 – followed suit in 1953 (Clark 1975). This 1100-bed hospital had all of its doors open night and day, although outer doors were locked at night. Warlingham Park Hospital was also open by 1954 except for two wards housing persistent absconders. At the same time, Dr E. S. Stern (1956) reported that Central Hospital, Hatton, 'was now completely open'. Fulbourn Hospital, Cambridge, opened its last permanently locked door in 1958, and Clark stated that in Great Britain 'many doors are now open' (Clark 1956, p.1007).

It is difficult to know just how many, for as Hurst observed, 'the method of unlocking wards has been expounded somewhat vaguely' (Hurst 1957, p.306). Unsurprisingly so, since the superintendents got on with the job. However a small number did publish (largely declarative) articles which attempted to say something about what they were trying to achieve and against what odds.

Preparation for change

Opinions about the groundwork needed to bring about change differed. Some asserted that satisfactory nurse–patient relationships were a prerequisite, as well as the courting of public opinion (O'Neil 1958; Stern 1956). Rees (1954), alternatively, was happy to boot through changes and present the open hospital as an accomplished fact. Koltes argued that 'patients must be encouraged towards the attitude that the hospital is theirs' (Koltes 1956, p.306), that improved behaviour inevitably follows attitudinal change and that this leads 'naturally' to the unlocking of doors. Bell (1955), however, believed that good nurse–patient relationships would only occur after the doors were open. Stern (1957) asserted that patients must be respected as persons and that paranoid hostility and potential absenteeism needed to be worn down by constant kindness.

Rees and Glatt (1955) advocated a more systematic approach involving habit and occupational training as a prelude to opening, and Hurst (1957) noted that Mapperley Hospital also favoured this approach. Stern (1957) had begun large-scale occupations for chronic patients as early as 1945, which aided enormously the process of discharging some of them into the community. These reforms proceeded quite well and, as we will see, it was only when their objective – unlocking the doors – actually materialised that problems began. For the nurses, the issue was about control and accountability.

Escape

Until the 1950s the most successful hospitals were those whose patients were kept in safe custody (Dingwall *et al.* 1988) so that by the late 1940s the social structure of hospitals had become rigid and repressive with patients held under restrictive rules of which 'the multiplication ad absurdum of suicide precautions was the most striking example' (Clark 1956, p.1005). Escapes were a serious matter and their ever-present threat a constant worry to the nurses. Rees described some conditions of 'escape': if during a pursuit a patient was lost sight of, even if subsequently sighted and apprehended, then this counted as an escape. So did a paroled patient who did not return at a predetermined time. Rees stated that this information was required in order 'to fix the responsibility for the escape' (Rees 1957, p.308).

At Fulbourn Hospital, nurses recalled that anyone held responsible for an escape was summarily dismissed. Snow (1959) noted how the nurses were very apprehensive about the consequences of accidents, suicides as well as escapes, and Barton (1976, p.50) provided an example of a charge-nurse who predicted all sorts of likely crimes committed by open door escapees.

Such forebodings being proved incorrect usually brought a reluctant acceptance of the newer methods. Rees, for instance, recalled a charge-nurse 'closely watching his little flock of gardening patients in dread lest one should walk off through the newly-opened gate' (Rees 1954, p.953). Informed that the responsibility, were this to happen, lay with the superintendent, 'the nurse's relief was patent and the whole atmosphere of the group changed' (Rees 1954, p.953).

Another superintendent, Arthur Bowen (1979), noted two distinct types of nursing attitudes towards him:

1. If the silly sod [i.e. Bowen] wants to open the doors well let him get on with it and take the consequences – it isn't our responsibility.

2. The anxiety-prone, obsessional and conscientious nurse who would (even) lurk by the newly opened door to make sure that nothing untoward happened and who would become increasingly anxious unless reassured.

Bowen (1988) has commented on the anxiety and consequent opposition of, particularly, long-serving nurses. Initially, the power of medical superintendents had been spectacular. By the 1950s, however, it was rarely absolute, and political skill was often required to bring about reform. Clark (1975) recalled the promises which had to be given to nurses as to who would 'carry the can' if patients escaped, and Stern (1957) described the anxieties of the nurses at the prospect of unrestrained patients.

Custodial nursing

Bott located the controlling function of mental hospitals with the medical superintendent, but commented that it was the nurses who 'immediately exercised it':

> The nursing staff regard themselves as being responsible for the control function…ultimately, though more tacitly, they regard themselves as responsible to the external society. (Bott 1976, p.127)

The primary task of the nurses, as they saw it, was to keep their ward and its residents clean, quiet and obedient: this they achieved within oppressive, militaristic and ultimately, for themselves as well as their charges, squalid, hopeless and unrelenting regimes. Everything was dominated by the clash of keys (Jones 1960; Koltes 1956). Bell (1955) stated that *had* nurses been consulted they would have opposed the opening of doors 'resolutely', and that for months after opening they continued, surreptitiously, to relock them. The tables were turned when Stern stealthily unlocked a door between two open male wards, at Hatton Hospital, saying that, 'The staff did not know that this was only the thin edge of the wedge; but I now literally had my foot in the door' (Stern 1957, p.577).

At Nabum and Bootham Park Hospitals, Bowen used an 'open letter' approach as a means of persuasion. Although the originals are lost, one of his letters re-surfaced in a commemorative paper and this is an extract:

> One of the interesting things about the history of the last couple of centuries or so has been the way in which fashions have waxed and waned. It is a curious thing that, despite the considerable advances that have been made, there does not seem to be any enduring or well-proven body of knowledge from which each generation makes fresh advances. Take, for example, the question of open doors in psychiatric hospitals. It was in the early part of the 1950s and slightly later that open doors were heralded as a revolutionary change in the therapeutic community; but in 1881 Dr Tuke in this country noted that the doors of Fyfe and Kinross had been open for ten years, and he remarked that 'liberty of action is no more controlled than in the wards of a general hospital'. Dr Cameron of the Midlothian Asylum, in the same year, said, 'It is now possible to traverse the entire building without requiring to use a key.' Dr Saxty Good at Littlemore Hospital in 1922 noted that security was best achieved not by locking doors but by patient–staff relationships. Yet now over recent years, in this country at least, one sees a return to the locked door system; various reasons are put forward, such as that it confers greater security upon the patient, or else that it is necessary for the safety of the large numbers of elderly people who now inhabit our hospitals. (Bowen 1979, p.540)

The letter is notable in its appeal to history: note, too, its 'apostolic function', the sense of people being led towards a different way of doing things.

Not all the nurses were anti-open door: some warmed to the new systems if they saw that it worked without too much disruption. At Mapperley Hospital, discussions between the nurses and the medical administration resulted in the new system working well (Macmillan 1956). According to William Stern:

> Now we find that those who were most doubtful at first are as enthusiastic as the rest of us. Of course we all had some anxiety then, and I sometimes feared that Operation Sesame might become Operation Pandora. But we never opened a ward until the staff were ready for it, and always left the final decision to the Sister or Charge Nurse. (Stern 1957, p.578)

Clark says that some charge-nurses *requested* that wards be unlocked, as a means of reducing the tension which constant vigilance of patients brought. He went on:

quite a lot of male nurses [at Fulbourn] knew about active therapy and wanted to get the hospital opened up. They wanted to try opening the doors and seeing if it would work. What they needed was somebody who had the courage to stand by them when things went wrong, as, of course, they inevitably did. (Clark 1964, p.43)

Legacies of fear and apprehension remained, however, and some nurses refused to participate at all. Such refusals were not always accepted: at Dingleton Hospital, Dr Bell issued orders when persuasion failed, and T.P. Rees summarily dismissed a charge-nurse who refused to open a locked gate (Clark 1964).

Some reasons for the nursing attitudes

Nurses' opposition was likely to be effective because of their numerical strength and close proximity, in time and space, to the patients. Nurses could claim some affinity with the miserable living conditions of patients, something which conferred a primitive moral standing that other professionals lacked. Their everyday association with these 'wet, violent, feckless and dirty irresponsibles' (Clark 1991) conferred upon them a standing within the hospital hierarchy overall. The level of that standing might be low, but it was the foundation upon which hospitals operated. Many nurses were also immigrants whose self-esteem, on arrival, would have been low (Greenslade 1992). Whilst nurse training offered an education of sorts (a means of increased social standing), it did not compensate for the low opinion in which mental nurses were held. In the late 1950s, Dr David Rice (1988) requested indoor lavatories for nurses' accommodation. East Sussex County Council responded by inquiring why 'those people' would *need* indoor lavatories. It appears that, for some, 'those people' were not perceived with any marked degree of difference from those in their care: both groups being seen as low priorities. Yet, from the nurses' viewpoint the lower status accorded hospitalised patients may have provided some compensation, a measure of heightening their self-regard.

In John's (1961) view, mental nurse training was inferior and resulted in a lack of familiarity with literature that might support change. Nurses, in her view, neither possessed the time (a 48-hour working week was still operational) nor the enthusiasm to attend to the new ideas then beginning to circulate. Many of John's nurses had spent years in the same institutions, having entered the service in the 1930s: those achieving seniority did so by experience, and many others were immigrants. The situation did not lend itself to scholarship. In fact, it rather favoured resistance to and, on occasions, the destruction of innovation and good practice.

The nature of the nursing care

Because of staff shortages there was often only one nurse to accompany patients into the airing courts or outside the hospital. Consequently, potentially 'destructive' patients would remain inside: females, particularly, were prone to be treated like this. Maddox (1957) found in one hospital, that 34 per cent of female and 17 per cent of male patients were in refractory wards. Many of these women were 'faulty', which means they were either incontinent, refusing to wear their clothes, or 'difficult to manage'. Individual nursing care was non-existent and, from a career viewpoint, probably undesirable. 'Good' nurses were regarded as those who kept patients clean, tidy and quiet (Clark 1991). Such nurses contained patients and integrated procedures which maintained 'sameness'. This was the way in which they built up the service years needed for appointment to charge-nurse, an indefinite process but deservedly known as 'filling dead men's shoes'.

Relationships between the different grades of hospital was complex, ill-defined but often subtle. A particular difficulty was the growing size of the hospitals which made it impossible for superintendents (or matrons) to visit more than a few wards each day. That being the case, long and complicated rules evolved as substitutes for the superintendent's or matron's absence. In general, rules – often contained in books, for example the 'bath book' – had the intended effect of intensifying an ambience of servitude. In many cases, the superintendent became a 'father-figure', a benevolent paternalist, idealised but feared and obviating any need for junior staff to assume responsibility themselves. Better to enforce the rules and retain some power by doing so. John (1961) thought that loss of control was what lay behind the refusal to unlock doors: she noted that whilst unlocking doors diversified nurses' responsibility, they preferred to control their wards instead. As Beardshaw (1981) observed, if released patients were allowed to inhabit a wider social context, then nursing control would inevitably diminish, and such control was seen as a necessary bulwark against fear of victimisation.

Fear

Such fears were genuine. Memories of the 1930s, with its widespread unemployment, were part of the social experience of many working-class people. At this time, nurses were mainly working class, and many were immigrants, so that their vulnerability was two-pronged. Every mental hospital had its half-mythical stories of summary dismissals handed down for trivialities. Fear was the spur: realisation that loss of job meant loss of everything; many nurses knew little other than hospital life; the working day was long and there were plenty of them; large numbers lived in hospital houses on or nearby hospital grounds in isolated areas; for some, long and complicated family ties existed within a single institution. Martin, at Claybury Hospital, observed that the nurse's:

> task must remain largely that of maintaining a relationship of authority and submission between himself and the patient. Failure on his part may, in fact or in fantasy, threaten him from above with loss of promotion or favour, and this strikes at his home life where promotion means material security. (Martin 1955, p.1190)

The occupational status of nurses was linked closely to their attitudes and beliefs about mental illness, the tendency being to see it as irredeemable and an ever present threat. That threat would materialise from unleashing either the patients' potentiality to violence or their desire to reproduce themselves and swamp decent society. Hence, a strict male/female segregation was imposed within the hospitals, extending to separate locking mechanisms for female and male wards, and the provision of punishments for losing one's key.

Reluctance to talk

In 1947 a Ministry of Health Working Party Report found 'the average intellectual calibre of the nursing staffs in mental hospitals to be significantly lower than in other types of hospital'. If true, it is hardly surprising that nurses were failing to conceptualise opening the doors as eliciting a variety of effects, rather seeing it as a single determining event: the single event being violence. Bott commented on how the nurse's:

> adherence to the control function showed itself in the content of the rumours that usually circulated when a ward was starting a new programme. The typical content of such rumours was that the patients were being allowed to indulge themselves sexually or to be violent, the two instinctual urges that is traditionally the task of society to keep under control. (Bott 1976, p.127)

Elizabeth Bott argued that the restrictive practices of hospitals were grounded in anxiety and when Clark *et al.* (1962) reported that nurses had 'little to say', they concluded that this was less to do with limited intellect and more to do with a deep-seated unease surrounding the abolition of ritual. What Clark *et al.* had observed was that during reorganisational crises, nurses (but not patients) remained obdurately silent and passive in the company of other professionals, only becoming verbally (usually negatively) communicative when in their own company. Ramon (1985) similarly noted that innovation was more disturbing for nurses than patients, and that they particularly resented the kinds of changes represented by therapeutic communities, since these *encouraged* criticisms from patients and violated traditional lines of authority. Most nurses were hamstrung because the institutions had bred custodialism in them, with a range of sanctions in place if slip-ups occurred: their consequent anxiety meant that articulating alternative viewpoints about psychiatric care was unlikely.

Open doors: basic orientations

Much of the open door debate took place in the *Lancet*, where a small number of hospital superintendents asserted their cause with great conviction. Readers were charged to 'open the doors of all mental hospitals forthwith' (Macmillan 1956, p.953). Bell was especially fervent, exulting over his achievements at Dingleton; 'A mental hospital without a single locked door anywhere! No locked doors for over four years!' (Bell 1955, p.42) and he denounced any colleagues who did not remove the 'barbarity' of locked doors immediately. For these writers, the open door was an end in itself, which meant that their reasoning behind it was often piecemeal and limited. Interestingly, none of the open door enthusiasts shunned physical treatments, nor did they challenge the bio-physical basis of mental illness, or call for a re-alignment of professional/patient relationships within hospital regimes. Rather, they were impelled by a basic goodwill towards their fellow man, and, in the main, the *Lancet* pronouncements on the open door reflect precisely that. They rarely extend beyond denouncing locked doors as incompatible with common decency, and curiously ignore what the changes might mean in respect of altering perspectives about mental illness.

Patients as persons

Whether 20th-century psychiatry represents the growing ascendancy of neuropathology or, alternatively, the Freudian unravelling of the human psyche, one outcome of a flourishing psychiatric profession was that more and more people were becoming suitable cases for treatment. One aspect of this was the 'one-hour session' becoming sacrosanct to the practice of psychiatric medicine, to the neglect of the other 23 hours of the patient's life (Bott 1976). It was Thomas Rees's view that developments in individual pathology, from whatever perspective, bypassed the lives of most hospitalised patients. For Rees, patients were entitled to a social life, to express their feelings and attitudes, and he sought to recapture for them something of the Moral Treatment of an earlier period. His *Lancet* article reflected an historical awareness referring back to Pinel and an Enlightenment which, he said, 'has gone on ever since and which is now gaining momentum' (Rees 1954, p.953).

A feature of Moral Treatment was a sharing in daily activities by staff and patients which was based on beliefs about goodness and redemption. Here lay the evangelical fervour of the superintendents to treat patients as fellow humans: it is said that Bell, at Dingleton, could not abide mentally ill people being locked up. The *Lancet* (1954) began to speak of containment as a 'literally maddening factor' and freedom as 'a powerful therapeutic agent'.

> Whatever differences of opinion may exist in regard to the advantages gained by the introduction of new drugs, one thing is clear: that the employment and, let me add, the repose of patients, well-ordered arrangements and the tact of the superintendent will often-times do more to reduce the amount of excitement and noise in an asylum than tons of chloral and bromide. (Winston 1962)

The above extract is from a speech by Daniel Hack Tuke in 1881 but, as Winston suggests, 'substitute barbiturates and chlorpromazine for the chloral and bromides and it might well have been written today' (Winston 1962, p.12).

A note about 'the drug explanation'

The psychoanalyst and anthropologist Elizabeth Bott (1976) recalls how, in the 1950s, she had tacitly accepted the prevailing psychiatric view that changes in psychiatric practice were caused by the introduction of tranquillising drugs. Indeed, from their inception, these drugs were hailed as a 'revolution in psychiatry', an assertion sustained for years by all but the most honest of commentators. Ramon (1988) suggests that it was the absence of an underlying theory to account for the 'open door' which allowed retrospective 'explanations' based on drugs to become credible. The drug explanation did supply a conceptual gap, but it also legitimised the role of medicine in psychiatry. In particular, pharmacological explanations made it possible to frame psychological disturbance within a linear cause/effect model, whilst minimising explanations based on social or psychological principles.

Desirable outcomes

Whatever the immediate causes, the results of unlocking wards are even less well-established, and claims and counter-claims must be viewed dispassionately. The belief that social improvement followed the opening of doors may well be a projection on the part of those responsible (Hurst 1957). Snow (1959) claimed that opening doors diminished tension between staff and patients, and Bell verified this: 'a complete lack of tension exists in both staff and patients compared with the days when all wards and corridors were locked' (Bell 1955, p.45). Stern also observed how 'The whole staff-patient relationship is transformed. Nurses are no longer regarded as turnkeys' (Stern 1957, p.578). John also thought that 'more liberty greatly influences the atmosphere of the working situation' (John 1961, p.13), and Cameron stated that 'a major result of setting up an open system was the immediate and profound effect upon staff/patients relationships' (Cameron 1950, p.87).

On a different tack, Bell (1955) noted a decrease in epileptic seizures, and Macmillan (1954) reported a drop in the levels of violence. Macmillan and Bell (1964) claimed that paranoid patients were less likely to abscond, and Hurst (1957) stated this finding for manic as well as paranoid patients at Shenley Hospital, St Albans. Macmillan and Bell also claimed that paranoid patients lost most of their hallucinations and became less deluded. Hurst (1957) corrected the mistaken assumption that well-integrated patients would be a high risk for absconding, as well as finding that known escapees absconded no more frequently when their wards were unlocked.

The main problem, according to Hurst (1957), was that of 'confused schizophrenics', although it was thought that routine occupation might help here. According to the *Lancet* (1954), senile patients were seen as presenting special difficulties due to their confusion, agitation and disorientation; they might wander off, lose their way, harm themselves or be found in a state of neglect or starvation. Stern (1957) also worried about 'wandering patients' and was careful not to unlock any doors adjacent to steep stairways.

Ratcliff examined these issues systematically, producing statistical comparisons between Dingleton and other Scottish Border hospitals for the ten years following the opening of the doors at Dingleton, and he concluded that:

> The open door regime proved as safe to the inpatients and the community as that in the other Scottish mental hospitals. The open door policy stimulated patients in the catchment area voluntarily to make fuller use of the hospital with apparent benefit. (Ratcliff 1962, p.6)

Undesirable outcomes

At Dingleton, Bell (1954) had provided a loose-structured environment with plenty of activities for patients, and in other places therapeutic activities were also implemented so as to dampen any anxieties brought about by unlocking the doors. That said, the provision of 'occupations' often seemed designed to act as an inducement to stay rather than for any intrinsic value they might possess: 'After all, why should a patient leave the only place where he can always be sure of a kind word and a sympathetic ear?' (Stern 1957, p.578).

Bott (1976) felt that occupational schemes make hospital life more pleasant, thus decreasing the desire to live in the outside world. Other tactics were more direct: 'at Warlingham Park there existed a reliable wire-mesh fence surrounding the hospital precinct and a porter at the gate' (Hurst 1957, p.308). Bickford reported 'open' wards with 50 'voluntary' patients whose only visits outside were well-escorted trips to hospital entertainments, or being '"turned out" into an airing court with a high iron railing and locked doors in it,' (Bickford 1955, p.423). He also noted activities which must have rendered the open door, in some places, absurd and humiliating:

> If the patients want to reach the grounds on the other side of the rails they have to go up an iron staircase from the court to their own ward, and then down a staircase from it to reach another ward. From this a passage leads to the main entrance, where a porter may be standing. (Bickford 1955, p.423)

Stern (1957) mused that it was possible to walk out of his hospital without a key but only if one possessed a knowledge of the design of the female side – a knowledge even many of the nurses did not possess. Hurst (1957) observed that, at Netheme Hospital, the grounds were open to the surrounding countryside, but that five locked wards were retained.

Clark (1975, p.24) states that unlocking doors was only sustained by vigorous treatment of absconders; small groups of troublesome patients were 'well tranquillised' and one report speaks of persistent absconders being leucotomised (Bell 1955, p.45). Somewhat more ingenious was the removal of a main gate at Friern Hospital and the implementation of a parole system, whereby patients' movements could be monitored. Under pressure from the Board of Control, these parole systems became widespread: trumpeted as a 'liberalisation', they could be seen as a more refined method of incarceration, and one of the mainstays of good patient management.

Surroundings

The relative population density surrounding the different hospitals, their degrees of urbanisation, was an important consideration. At Dingleton, where all doors were unlocked in 1948, relationships with the surrounding townsfolk were good. More importantly, the adjacent town, Melrose, was small and rural (population 2000) and a determined and comprehensive courting of private and public agencies worked to good effect (Bell 1955). The townspeople were proud of their hospital and not afraid to send their relatives for treatment. Such cosiness would prove more difficult in densely populated areas. The problems posed by a 418-bedded hospital, at Dingleton, may have been more easily solved than in much larger hospitals (Roberts 1967). Ratcliff (1962), however, points out that Dingleton was the only NHS mental hospital in the Scottish Borders and so was required to accept all of its referrals whether certified or voluntary. During 1950–1959, he goes on, no patient was refused on 'difficult to manage' grounds and no patient was moved because unsuitable for open door conditions. Indeed, Bell (1955) was sensitive to the charge that he administered a small hospital, and stated that he had previously administered a 1000-bed hospital; having visited it recently, he could see no reason why it could not also be unlocked. Some of the open hospitals *were* large: Central Hospital, Hatton, for example, had 1830 beds with all wards open, no main gates and a river and railway nearby (Stern 1956).

However, even Bell conceded that in urban areas most hospitals will need to lock two or three wards and Clark (1956) expressed similar fears in respect of urban areas. Rees (1957) adroitly pointed out that treatment depends on the levels of toleration shown by a society to its deviants and more helpless members.

Bowen (1988) believed that open door policies depended on the cultural setting within which they occurred. He administered two hospitals which differed not just in geography but also by cultural tradition. Bootham Park Hospital (formerly the York Lunatic Asylum founded in 1777, but latterly a private hospital) and Nabum Hospital (formerly York City Mental Hospital founded in 1906) differed, in that Bootham Park owed much to the Scottish Chartered Hospitals in its standards of care and the liberal outlook of its nursing staff. Nabum was a more traditional hospital, and Bowen's first impression was of a locked system, enclosed and inward looking. He quickly realised that the problem was not just about removing locks but of coming to grips with the staff's apprehensions of the consequences of this.

Other manoeuvres

Bickford suspected that some open hospitals had made arrangements whereby, prior to opening, difficult patients would be transferred out of them. In addition, he believed that open doors were irrelevant to long-standing patients, stating that although less repressed, a patient is not necessarily more free because a door is open, and that the open door might become an alternative to active treatment:

> Every advance may be the enemy of the next, and today there is a danger that open wards and voluntary patients will come to be regarded as an acceptable substitute for treatment. (Bickford 1958, p.424)

He also argued that:

> To be confined to an unlocked ward is less repressive than to be confined to a locked one, but nobody should imagine that a patient is necessarily free just because his ward door is not locked. (Bickford 1958, p.423)

Specifically, a non-treated schizophrenic patient may deteriorate as much in an open as in a closed system. Although incessant, Bickford's precautionary tone echoed that of some of his contemporaries. Even the most liberal superintendents had doubts and Clark's (1956) description of the period as 'an experimentation' reflects uncertainty and thus hesitancy.

A locked door by any other name

Of further concern was the possibility of open door substitutions such as overmedicating patients or keeping them unnecessarily in their beds. Keeping patients in bed (or in pyjamas) had been a timeworn response to problem patients, especially during periods of low staffing. Hunter and Macalpine recorded the following comments of the Board of Control at Friern Hospital in 1941:

> At the time of our visit there were 87 male and 116 female patients under treatment in bed: that is, 9 per cent and 11 per cent respectively of the patients in residence. Only five of the 87 men were regarded as being in bed on account of mental symptoms, whereas 60 per cent of the women in bed were so regarded. (Hunter and Macalpine 1974, p.162)

Bickford caustically referred to 'the open ward where ten or more of the patients are always to be found in bed because otherwise they would run away' (Bickford 1958, p.423).

Towards the close of the 1950s Mullane (1960), a visiting examiner for the General Nursing Council, observed that a refined but still rigorous custodialism prevailed. In one hospital the open door operated in conjunction with the (by now) widespread use of graduated parole systems:

Stage 1: Parole within the area of the male wards but not to enter the female ward areas (or vice versa).

Stage 2: Parole within the hospital grounds.

Stage 3: Parole beyond the grounds.

In a second hospital, Mullane observed that outside doors of all wards were open in daytime, allowing free access to the ward courts. These courts, however, were completely enclosed by railings, walls and locked gates. About 38 patients (approximately 6 per cent of the hospital population) had obtained permission to venture beyond the courts and about 10 could go as far as the local shops once every week. In a third hospital, she found a selective parole whereby most patients were free to come and go as they pleased during the day, but with unsuitable patients 'instructed to remain indoors'.

Change of heart or change of concept

It is interesting to speculate – in the light of impending 1960s radicalism – on whether open door initiatives reflected changes in beliefs about the nature of mental illness. The *Lancet's* (1954) view was that if locked up patients see their doctors and nurses as gaolers, then therapy will be transformed by unlocking the doors. Reference is also made to a 'consciousness of captivity', which predisposes patients to behave in ways that are normally accounted for by reference to 'their illness'. Macmillan (1956) believed that what was still regarded by many as psychotic behaviour was really a consequence of man-made restrictions, deprivation of personal amenities and incarceration. For Bell (1954), open doors uncovered the real illness, uncomplicated by symptoms induced by confinement, frustration and resentment which had previously been interpreted as psychosis.

An important overlap of the Fifties and the Sixties occurred when Maxwell Jones took over from George Bell at Dingleton Hospital. Although Bell had been at the forefront of the open door movement, Jones was not impressed with his inheritance:

When I came to take up my post at Dingleton Hospital in December 1962, I found the traditional hierarchical structure of a 400 bed British mental hospital. My predecessor, Dr George Bell and the Matron, Miss Mullen, both perceived their roles in terms of status and authority. (Jones 1982, p.11)

This represents the beginnings of a critique of institutional authority which marks the difference between the essential paternalism of the 1950s reforms and the more radical shifts which lay ahead. Needless to say, these shifts would occur within a comparatively small number of places only. None of the new therapeutic communities had to cope with the huge numbers of patients, with their wide array of dysfunctions, which was the lot of the NHS mental hospital. As we shall see, attempts were made to implement therapeutic community practice within some of the hospitals, but it was to prove difficult and, right up to their demise, the hospitals retained their custodial mindset: a mindset now transferred into an 'asylum in the community' with proposed stringent legislation to compel treatments without hospitalisation. We may also note the increasing emphasis on locked forensic psychiatric units, where custodialism is legitimated (by law) far more effectively than in the past. Barham (1997), discussing the implications of the 1996 Mental Health (Patients in the Community) Act, notes that it shies away from actual compulsory treatment – but which is currently being proposed – whilst allowing for patients to be 'conveyed' to any place where they can be 'treated, occupied or educated'. In favour of compulsion is the argument that it will only apply to small numbers of patients 'at risk', and that coercion is needed here if the public are to be persuaded that community care works to manage people with mental health problems. Pragmatism, of course, has always attended psychiatric practice: hatching compromises, for instance, between psychiatry and the state, whereby humane treatments are implemented with the proviso that psychiatry will also safeguard society by 'policing' difficult patients. Peter Morrall (1998) insists that psychiatry and, particularly, psychiatric nurses – into whose hands the practicalities will fall – should 'come clean' and acknowledge their policing function, acknowledge that it is necessary and right, and stop ignoring this difficult issue. He does have a point. However, he underplays the conflict that practitioners experience when trying to reconcile regulatory functions with their claims to person-centred care: indeed, therapists are entitled to give some allegiance to their clients. Working for the State only complicates matters: it doesn't resolve moral dilemmas. Part of the problem is defining what is meant by coercion, reconciling notions of coercion with 'duty to care' in ways that might find some agreement. Conventional psychiatry has indeed avoided the problem, sporadically engaging with critics such as Thomas Szasz (1994), whilst smugly relying on its own self-assurance. That is why the dilemma of the open door will persist in different guises and – acknowledged or not – psychiatry will continue to police people whom other agencies of the State cannot understand or tolerate.

References

Barham, P. (1997) *Closing the Asylum: The Mental Patient in Modern Society.* Harmondsworth: Penguin Books.

Barraclough, B. (1986) 'In conversation with David Clark: parts 1 and 2.' *Bulletin of the Royal College of Psychiatrists* (March and April), 42–49 (part 1), 70–75 (part 2).

Barton, R. (1976) *Institutional Neurosis,* 3rd edn. Bristol: John Wright.

Beardshaw, V. (1981) *Conscientious Objectors at Work.* London: Social Audit.

Bell, G.M. (1954) *Lancet* (6 November), 953–954.

Bell, G.M. (1955) 'A mental hospital with open doors.' *International journal of Social Psychiatry 1* (Summer), 42.

Bickford, J.A.R. (1955) 'The forgotten patient.' *Lancet* (29 October), 917–918.

Bickford, J.A.R. (1958) 'Shadow and substance: some changes in the mental hospital.' *Lancet* (22 February), 423–424.

Bott, E. (1976) 'Hospital in society.' *British Journal of Medical Psychology 49,* 97–140.

Bowen, A. (1979) Letter written in Millbank Memorial Fund.

Bowen, A. (1988) Personal correspondence.

Cameron, D.E. (1950) 'An open psychiatric hospital.' *Modern Hospital 74* (February), 84–88.

Clark, D.H. (1956) 'Functions of the mental hospital.' *Lancet* (17 November), 1005–1009.

Clark, D.H. (1964) *Administrative Therapy.* London: Tavistock Publications.

Clark, D.H. (1975) *Social Therapy in Psychiatry.* New York: Jason Aronson.

Clark, D.H. (1991) 'Maxwell Jones and the mental hospitals.' *International Journal of Therapeutic Communities 7,* (2 and 3), 117–123.

Clark, D.H., Hooper, D.F. and Oram, E.G. (1962) 'Creating a therapeutic community in a psychiatric ward.' *Human Relations 15,* 2, 123–147.

Dingwall, R., Rafferty, A.M. and Webster, C. (1988) *An Introduction to the Social History of Nursing.* London: Routledge.

Gostin, L. (1977) *A Human Condition Vol 1.* London: MIND.

Greenslade, L. (1992) 'White skins: white masks: mental illness and the Irish in Britain.' In P. O'Sullivan (ed) *The Irish Worldwide: History, Heritage, Identity Vol 2.* London: Leicester University Press.

Hunter, R. and Macalpine, I. (1974) *Psychiatry for the Poor: 1851 Colney Hatch Asylum Friern Hospital.* London: Dawsons of Pall Mall.

Hurst, L.C. (1957) 'The unlocking of wards in mental hospitals.' *American Journal of Psychiatry 114* (October), 306–308.

John, A. (1961) *A Study of the Psychiatric Nurse.* Edinburgh: Livingstone.

Jones, K. (1960) *Mental Health and Social Policy.* London: Routledge and Kegan Paul.

Jones, M. (1982) *The Process of Change.* London: Routledge and Kegan Paul.

Koltes, J.A. (1956) *American Journal of Psychiatry 108* (September), 250.

Macmillan, D. (1954) 'The unlocked door.' *Lancet* (6 November), 953–954.

Macmillan, D. (1956) 'Open doors in mental hospitals.' *International Journal of Social Psychiatry 2* (Autumn), 152–154.

Maddox, H. (1957) 'The work of mental nurses.' *Nursing Mirror* (19 April), 189–190.

Martin, D.V. (1955) 'Institutionalisation.' *Lancet* (3 December), 1188–1190.

Ministry of Health (1947) *The Recruitment and Training of Nurses.* Working Party Report. London: HMSO.

Morrall, P. (1998) *Mental Health Nursing and Social Control.* London: Whurr.

Mullane, E. (1960) 'Programme of resocialisation at Roundway hospital, Devizes, Wiltshire.' *Nursing Mirror* (8 July), 3–4.

O'Neil, F.J. (1958) 'Laying the foundations for an open mental hospital.' *Mental Hospitals* (9 February), 10–12.

Ramon, S. (1985) *Psychiatry in Britain: Meaning and Policy.* London: Croom Helm.

Ramon, S. (1988) 'Community care in Britain.' In A. Lavender and F. Holloway (eds) *Community Care in Practice.* New York: John Wiley.

Ratcliff, R.A.W. (1962) 'The open door: Ten year's experience in Dingleton.' *Lancet* (28 July), 188–190.

Rees, T.P. (1954) 'The unlocked door.' *Lancet* (6 November), 953–954.

Rees, T.P. (1957) 'Back to moral treatment and community care.' *Journal of Mental Science 103*, 303–313.

Rees, T. and Glatt, M.M. (1955) 'The management of a chronic ward in a mental hospital.' *The Practitioner 175*, 62–65.

Rice, D. (1988) Personal correspondence.

Roberts, N. (1967) *Mental Health and Mental Illness.* London: Routledge and Kegan Paul.

Rossetti, D.G. (1863) [1961] 'Sudden Light.' in O. Doughty (ed) *Poems.* London: J.M. Dent.

Snow, H.B. (1959) 'Open ward policy at St. Lawrence state hospital.' *American Journal of Psychiatry 105*, 779–789.

Stern, E.S. (1956) 'Open doors in mental hospitals.' *International Journal of Social Psychiatry 2* (Autumn), 152–154.

Stern, E.S. (1957) 'Operation sesame.' *Lancet* (16 March), 577–578.

Szasz, T. (1994) *Cruel Compassion: Psychiatric Control of Society's Unwanted.* Chichester: Wiley.

Winston, F. (1962) 'Beyond the open door.' *Mental Hygiene xivi* (1) (January), 11–19.

CHAPTER 5

Critiquing the Therapeutic Community

To walk into some places styled therapeutic communities is to experience a despairing realisation that one is in the midst of people who for the most part are lost in their own outer worlds and the outer worlds of others. They live in a sterile emptied out form of group existence.

David Cooper (1967)

Two streams

Had therapeutic communities started in the 1960s, not the decade before, they would have been called communes: more than likely, too, they would have positioned themselves on the periphery of mainstream psychiatry, or outside it. The 1950s, though, were less self-absorbed, so that the beginnings of therapeutic communities within existing mental institutions seem less surprising because of this. How ironic that mental hospitals were the springboard from which so much innovation – community psychiatric nursing, day hospitals, therapeutic communities – took off, and at a time when these same hospitals had started to decline. Odd too, that history has seen fit to demarcate hospital and community psychiatric practice, as though the latter represented all that is good, with the former seen as redolent of bad practice and even wrongdoing (Martin 1984). It is a view that has persisted, with a disproportionate interest in acute and community psychiatric provision to the neglect of long-stay, institutionalised, patients.

Having said that, the arrival of therapeutic communities challenged institutional practices: these communities sought to transform patients' lives by introducing a social dimension in the management of psychiatric disturbance. The dominant assumption was that:

Psychopathology was related to stressful environments...and that *so called* [my italics] sick people could be helped to look at and change their behaviour. The positive value of the social milieu was indicated, and a new avenue of inquiry opened up, through which the depersonalised social systems of hospitals were in some cases altered to become one of the tools of therapy. (Jansen 1980, p.14)

Accordingly, said Maxwell Jones:

We attempt to absorb the patient into the Unit community which has developed a definite culture of its own. This culture is maintained and perpetuated through the staff rather than through the patients, though in practice it is difficult to separate these two groups in the community. As far as possible, social and vocational roles are provided for while still in hospital. These roles approximate as far as possible to what is found in the relatively healthy outside community. (Jones 1952, p.xv)

The Henderson Hospital – of which Jones was director – became the flagship for this type of therapeutic community and it came to represent, in psychiatric circles, the archetypal community.

At the same time, the relevance of psychoanalytic thinking to the development of therapeutic communities is also important. In fact, the concept of therapeutic community evolved from these two separate but related streams. The communities of Main (1946) and Bion (1961), for instance, were primarily psychoanalytic in nature with the therapist occupying a central – interpretative – role. This stream led to the kind of psychoanalytic community represented by the Cassel Hospital. In Hinshelwood's (1999) view, therapeutic communities *originate* from psychoanalysis since, to begin with, they were about working out how to apply psychoanalysis in social settings. For Hinshelwood, that therapeutic communities constitute a culture of inquiry in their members stems from psychoanalysis which is, he says, just such a culture. As such, psychoanalysis continues to inform community practice, in its capacity to comprehend social settings (Hinshelwood 1999, p.42).

Where, however, psychoanalytic comprehension is transformed to implementation, then things fare less well. For instance, the abuses of human rights which accompanied the application of psychoanalytic principles at the Marlborough Day Hospital have been documented by Baron (1987): her account of the day-to-day requests of uncomprehending patients being analysed out of existence does not make pretty reading. The success of psychoanalysis at the Cassel Hospital, alternatively, is probably due to this particular clientele 'lending itself' to it. Speaking of the Cassel, Hinshelwood observes how its structure allows 'individual psychoanalytic psychotherapy to be conducted within the context of a living-together community: this dual track approach keeps the individual work rather separate from the community' (Hinshelwood 1999, p.45).

We will return to Hinshelwood's concerns about the 'appropriate' juncture of individual and social process in Chapter 8.

For now, I would suggest that the first stream, represented by the Henderson Hospital (Jones 1952, 1953, 1968, 1980) became the template for most forays into therapeutic community practice in Britain. Jones came from the Maudsley tradition of clinical psychiatry, not psychoanalysis, and his work was orientated towards a social construction of psychiatric practice. Thus, from early on, important differences emerged between his position and that of Main and Bion, who construed the determinants of behaviour largely from an individual psychopathology.

Notwithstanding these differences (maybe because of them), 1950s British psychiatry thrived, with all kinds of changes and experiments taking place. For example, drawing from both Jones and psychoanalysis, Tom Main asserted the significance of social systems via the occurrence of change through group analysis (Bion 1961; Foulkes 1964). For Main the hospital was:

> a social system based not on the medical model of a healthy knowledge-able staff and sick obedient patients, but upon the joint recognition of each individuals' capacity and limitations for performing essential tasks and with participation by all in allowing that these be carried out. (Main 1980, p.53)

Plainly, the concept of illness as inborn and irredeemable becomes suspect here and we may inquire how this came about. Social experiments in psychiatry were not new and had even been seen as resounding successes: the York Retreat is perhaps the best known. But such departures never became part of mainstream psychiatric provision. Initially, the Victorian asylums tried to capture something of the quality of the York experiment, but by the mid-1950s the asylums – now designated hospitals – had become grossly overcrowded, hopelessly institutionalised (Barton 1957; Martin 1955) and shrouded in an ideology of mental illness as essentially hereditary and in need of medical cure.

Social studies

What changed was the coming of the Second World War. It was this, above all, which lent weight to the notion of mental illness as neither inborn nor irredeemable. War-induced psychological distress brought recognition that many of those affected had previously functioned quite well, that biology alone could not account for their distress. The therapeutic community began when Maxwell Jones deduced from this that social learning experiences could be a means of unravelling – perhaps even reversing – what had happened to these soldiers.

At the same time, a (largely American) literature (Barton 1957; Belknap 1956; Caudill 1958; Dunham and Weinberg 1960; Greenblat et al. 1957; Martin 1955; Stanton and Schwartz 1954) was examining social relationships within hospitals, and showing how these could affect people living and working within them. In particular, this literature identified how tensions within staff groups could induce nervousness and apprehension amongst patients, and this armed reformers with much needed theoretical ammunition. For it was at this time that advances in physical treatments were also emerging. A number of anti-psychotic drugs were found to have beneficial effects with schizophrenic patients, and electric treatment was being used to eliminate depression in potentially suicidal patients. It might not have seemed a propitious time to engage in social experiments in the mental hospital system. But fuelled by a post-war climate of 'winds of change', and armed with an exciting social psychiatric literature, the therapeutic community movement got confidently underway.

Problems of definition

Trauer (1984) noted the many debates to which the new communities gave rise. For one thing, definitions flowed thick and fast as their advocates sought to stabilise the new approach partly as an entity which would sustain therapy, but also to promote research which would define mental illness as socially determined. It quickly transpired that an agreed definition was unlikely and it was this difficulty – to define terms – which impeded research. Surprisingly quickly, therapeutic communities came to mean different things, their wide variety of meanings leading to vague, misleading or euphemistic conclusions (Wilmer 1958a).

Of course, Jones (1953) had always contended that the therapeutic community was not a specific social system within which – and only within which – people could be cured. The problem was that as different varieties and methods evolved, each sought to develop its own (sometimes tortuous) terminology. An added difficulty was that accounts tended to come either from practitioners or from critics not put off by its imprecise constructs. Denber (1960) thought that imprecision *enhanced* the sense of freedom and democracy which the new departures represented. Abroms (1969) agreed, describing therapeutic communities as benevolent systems which fostered wide-ranging approaches to people's ills. Towell (1975) likewise saw communities not so much as treatment centres but as 'a kind of humanising ideology', where people's problems could be discussed and helped. Zeitlyn (1967), however, was having none of it. A contemporary of Maxwell Jones, he had a way of turning debate on its head. For him, therapeutic communities were failing to specify their treatment outcomes against the placebo effects of basic enthusiasm and vigour. Zeitlyn's humorous debunking of some communities makes for enjoyable reading (even now) and, looking back, it is surprising how uncomplicatedly some therapeutic community enthusiasts spoke of its positive effects; asserting, for instance, that if a benevolent ideology prevailed – whatever that might mean – people would respond by getting better.

And yet, however vague they might be, the search for community definitions pre-empts our current fascination with working out how practice is supported from evidence. There are differences of course. Earlier descriptions were about matching practice with theory, whereas today, political/economic pressures have forced psychiatry into the court of quantitatively measuring client interventions and linking these to outcomes. In the case of therapeutic communities, the dice would always be stacked against studies seeking to identify precise interventions: it was the community which would be doctor. In a sense, ends and means were collapsed into each other, and however real this was in everyday practice, it would always be hard to articulate communal processes in ways that outsiders could easily comprehend.

Patterns of research

Attempts to understand therapeutic communities through research followed two patterns. A small number were small-scale explorations of measurable attributes, such as community meetings (Maratos and Kennedy 1974; Trauer 1979, 1980) or ward atmosphere (Moos 1974). General formulations were more typical, for example Robert Rapoport's (1960) study, or research derived from systems theories (Marohn 1970). Although of limited applicability, the latter were often well-written and possessed an elegant appeal, particularly to those interested in playing down medical treatments or emphasising the benefits of social interaction. Rees (1957), for example, drawing from the World Health Organisation's Third Report (1953), suggested that:

> The most important single factor in the efficacy of the treatment given in a mental hospital appears to be...an intangible element which can only be described as its atmosphere. (Rees 1957, p.310)

As things progressed, some therapeutic community writing became romantic, philosophical, occasionally dramatic. Others, though, were less idealistic and more concerned to provide clearer accounts. For example, Wilmer (1958a) listed the following as important elements of good community practice:

- facilities
- patient sample
- staff
- therapy
- research/evaluation
- legal status.

Check-list approaches like these were used to compare therapeutic units, finding clear differences between some but at the same time discovering some unifying features as well. Overall, the central process observed was one of socialisation achieved through patients and staff sensing 'fellowship within the community'. Implicit in this fellowship was a feeling of mutual responsibility with relatively free and full communications, continuous feedback of information and endless observations by community members.

The charismatic leader

It was Carstairs and Heron's (1957) opinion that differences between units did not reflect alternative approaches so much as the contagious enthusiasm of their leaders. It *is* ironic that to further the goals of egalitarian communities, strong leadership was required. Sir Aubrey Lewis (an early, ambivalent, admirer of Maxwell Jones) was one of those who wanted to know 'how much was the method and how much was the man'. In the version of therapeutic community produced by David Clark called *Administrative Therapy*, there was a frank acknowledgement of a centralising role: 'the manipulation, modification, and constant scrutiny of the relationships spreading out from the administrator with the aim of controlling their effect on the patients' (Clark 1964, p.806).

Here, the administrator – medical superintendent – establishes the atmosphere of the hospital and sets the patterns for its day-to-day administration. Crockett (1960) rejected the top-down implications of this, saying that much supportive administration could be done by lay persons; he further asserted that administrative therapy was inconsistent with the notion of a flattened authority structure. Yet it seems that some arbitrary force was needed – as a kick start – to flatten hospital hierarchies, and Maxwell Jones saw no inconsistency in unilaterally decreeing that democracy ruled. The particular contexts from which different accounts emerged is very important: Clark, for instance, administered a large hospital whilst Jones presided over a much smaller unit. Stuart Whiteley (1990) attributed the success of therapeutic communities to Maxwell Jones's socioanalytic beliefs, and this is probably true for some types of communities. Most descriptions of therapeutic communities are indebted to him and his position is now summarised:

- Relationships within the community are held to be conducive to positive change when similar in form and structure to the outside world.

- Patients become agents in defining the terms by which they may change consistent with the ordinary demands of society.

- The entire community sees itself as therapeutically relevant especially through regular group meetings. Alternatively, interactions may not be premeditated but be no less therapeutic for all that.

- The hierarchical system is 'flattened' so that all may share in the decision making of the unit as well as its responsibilities.

- The freeing of communication systems is held to be important and as little as possible in the way of roles, tradition and structure may stand in the way of free and full discussion.

Communicating and meeting

In respect of the last point, Stanton and Schwartz (1954) showed how covert communications amongst staff could produce tension amongst patients; therefore, they argued, staff must acknowledge internal conflicts and try to resolve them, probably in open communication within mixed (patients and staff) groups. Their book *The Mental Hospital* was very influential and Jones seized its emphasis on communication when working out his approach:

It would seem to me that in any mental organisation conflicting feelings must be recognised and, if possible, dealt with otherwise a situation arises where staff cannot handle their own interpersonal difficulties and this is a contradiction in terms. (Jones 1980, p.115)

Shoenberg (1980) saw this 'opening up' as fundamental to community development although she knew that it would be difficult to achieve. Ramon (1985) went further and thought these new communities actually threatened staff (especially the nurses), involving as they did a blurring of patient/ therapist boundaries. Gunna Dietrich – a noted nurse educator at the time – commented (1976) that nurses' training 'is geared towards suppressing any show of emotion in themselves and in their patients'. In addition, psychiatric nurses also resisted changes to the social organisation of their wards and working practices. Within medical circles, undercurrents of scepticism also accompanied change: James Bickford (1958) challenged the validity of many of the changes although his incessant recriminations lost their edge over time. Zeitlyn (1967) was more specific (and witty) in dismissing group work as a treatment and others were equally unimpressed. Eventually, however, most mental hospitals absorbed at least some of the tenets of therapeutic community practice and throughout the 1950s, 1960s, and 1970s anti-institutionalisation grew apace, particularly directed towards the cruder aspects of custodialism.

It is worth remembering, as Martin (1984) shows, that the lives of most hospitalised patients still left much to be desired. Celebrating the 1950s flourishing of social-psychiatry can deflect from the broader, more uneven, picture. Whilst therapeutic communities made their mark, other mental hospitals lay dormant and practically unaccounted for until the spate of government inquiries which began towards the end of the Sixties, and which laid bare a catalogue of misery, deprivation and abuse. Moreover, the attention paid to the virtuoso communities may have worked to camouflage more widespread custodial/punitive practices. Thus, a concept of therapeutic communities as 'tokenism' becomes plausible with psychiatry being construed as bits of excellence strewn here and there against a background that is much more variable.

Meetings

In the opinions of most commentators, group meetings were central to therapeutic community practice. For Shoenberg, the meeting was the only feature not requiring change or revision and that 'most agree that the quality and depth of community experience, and therefore of what can be achieved, appears to relate to the number of meetings' (Shoenberg 1980, p.68).

Of course therapeutic communities were small and fairly homogeneous in terms of patient population. Much of the seminal literature (Main 1946; Stanton and Schwartz 1954) stemmed from small neurosis units like the Cassel Hospital in Britain and Chestnut Lodge in the USA, and it is hardly surprising that larger institutions experienced difficulties when exposed to the new ideas. In the fullness of time, Dennis Martin would introduce therapeutic community practice within a large setting, Claybury Hospital, and David Clark, at Fulbourn Hospital, did likewise, but these were exceptions: most hospitals settled for modified forms of therapeutic community, the unlocking of doors being their most visible aspect.

In Rossi and Filstead's (1973) view, the size (of organisation) did not matter since the concept refers to a method of organising a social system and not a specific unit of analysis. There is something in this, and introducing therapeutic community principles into some of the big hospitals did improve things. But it is in the sense of small groups of people with similar concerns that we think of as classical therapeutic community. Small units permit levels of group cohesion not easily achieved in larger organisations. The kind of intimacies described by Garnett and Schlunke (1984) at London's Arbours Clinic, for instance, would be impossible in anything but a small unit. Called a 'naturalistic household' by Manning (1989), the Arbours is a place where patients are enabled to regress to earlier stages of their development so as to begin processes of re-growth and change and this clearly implies small, protected, meeting paces. It also, however, suggests an element of furtiveness as we discussed in the Historical Preface where the therapeutic community's most famous case of regression turned out to be something quite different.

Clark's divisions

Clark's (1965) separation of therapeutic communities into 'approach' and 'proper' conceded that therapeutic community 'proper' was just not workable in institutions housing large numbers of patients with diverse psychiatric disorders. For Clark, an 'approach' which aimed to restructure the hospital patient's day – and treat patients as individuals wherever possible – was preferable because it was more workable. An important difference between this approach and Jones's model was the relative contribution which patients would make to each other's treatment, what Stubbledine (1960) called the 'universality of therapeutic potential'. Clark, however, was able to figure out what would work in a large hospital: he surmised that communal management was a non-starter. Attempting to provide empirical support for Clark's position, Manning (1979) analysed eight British communities and found patterns which were roughly consistent with it. Further work by Price and Moos (1975) also supported the concept of a therapeutic community 'proper' as a function of the amount and nature of patient participation. Participation, of course, relates to the kinds of patients involved: communities like the Henderson had an ideology of treatment which prescribed which patients would benefit. The problem for the bigger hospitals was that in trying to utilise social psychiatric principles they also had to cope with hundreds of patients with diverse illnesses. They were helped by the fact of social changes and growing concerns about living conditions in the hospitals. The Report of the World Health Organisation (1953) had not mentioned patient involvement any more than it did group meetings, or the social analysis of day-to-day events, but its recommendations concerning rehabilitative and re-socialisation programmes eventually won support. Even sceptics like Zeitlyn (1967) could see the advantages of general social/therapeutic change. But he believed that Clark's distinction between 'proper' and 'approach' was rarely maintained in practice and that the supposed differences were impossibly blurred by ambiguous language. Mischievously quoting Maxwell Jones:

> All that is intended is that the (therapeutic community) should mobilise the interest, skill, and enthusiasm of staff and patients and give them sufficient freedom of action to create their own optimal treatment and living conditions. (Jones 1967, p.1093)

Zeitlyn concluded that this constituted a standpoint of such generalised proportions as to suggest that there is no 'proper' therapeutic community at all.

The proper community

In 1960 Robert Rapoport and his team produced a report of the Henderson Unit which was to have far-reaching conclusions. In general, their report was critical but in the process it gave 'The Therapeutic Community' a language and a reputation which would characterise it indelibly. Specifically, they crystallised four themes which, in their view, defined the overall workings of the Henderson.

1. Democratisation. Each member shares equally in the exercise of power.

2. Permissiveness. Tolerance of deviant or abnormal behaviour without suppression whilst still being able to react to it with understanding.

3. Communalism. All events in the unit are shared experiences with full participation and openness.

4. Reality confrontation. People's behaviours are reflected back to them in an open and honest fashion by others, thus avoiding the distance and artificiality of analytic, expert or interpretative comments.

These principles caught the imagination of many and in the rush to embrace them as 'truths', it was overlooked that Rapoport (1960) had also indicated problematic issues (never fully resolved) surrounding them. The report's cautious approval of the unit's activities disappointed Jones. According to Jones's successor, Stuart Whiteley (1990, p.27), Rapoport, taken as whole, 'demonstrated that the method was not an overall alternative to orthodox theories'. The Henderson staff spoke of contradictions and qualifications; democratisation, for instance, was not synonymous with political equality, and permissiveness did not indicate sexual license. Of course, the lack of definitional clarity that Rapoport noted is not surprising if one considers that therapeutic communities may have started to 'act into' their growing reputation for begetting bohemian values. Conflicts about what constituted psychotherapeutic 'treatment' on the one hand and 'socio-rehabilitation' on the other, were to bedevil therapeutic communities for years, and particularly where there were suspicions of violating moral norms. For some, experiments in living – masquerading as 'medical treatment' – were a dubious proposition to begin with and always to be shunned.

Justification by ideology

The details of Rapoport's (1960) investigation became lost to followers of therapeutic community practice, many of whom embraced the four principles with self-conscious moral fervour. 'Democratisation', for example, acquired such exalted status that, as David Kennard (1979) observed, 'the slightest suspicion of hierarchy was viewed with disgust'. The therapeutic community literature began to glow with accounts of its own progress: negative reports were few. Such easy acceptance fitted the anti-scepticism of the times but of course it also prevented the kinds of cost benefit analysis which might have showed how effective the process was and for whom. True, the business of tying psychiatric interventions to efficacy was light years away and although such concepts would eventually win some adherents, the nature of therapeutic community practice was hardly susceptible to quantitative analysis. Advocates of evidence-based practice unsurprisingly favour interventions that yield objective outcomes. In a sense, the therapeutic community could never be like that, no more than any system which accounts experience as an end in itself. Instead, therapeutic communities engaged in endless self-examination to the point where such rumination bred self-doubt: there even occurred, in some communities, a penchant for discussing their own demise, with community 'oscillations' defined as the seeds of destruction. Whilst psychologically fascinating, such preoccupations are 'anti-researchable' since their communication is only meaningful to and of itself. To try to present a 'seeds of destruction' mentality to external agencies in abstract form (i.e. as results) would defeat the (half-realised) 'purposes' of community oscillations, which are inherent in the ongoing experiences of the community; the 'research' is, in essence, unknowable outside of the experiencing community.

The 1970s and onwards

By the late 1970s, Crockett (1978) had embarked upon a review of therapeutic communities so as to reformulate their characteristics more precisely. Determined to examine the extent to which community practice matched public claims he found (with considerable variation) that the main tenets of communities were:

Size
It is small enough for each member to know one another.

Community meetings
Often daily, these involve all who live and work in the community.

Psychodynamic and psychosocial theory
The belief that psychiatric problems are a product of psychodynamic conflict and/or social pressures.

Analysis of events
Continual attempts are made to understand the social and dynamic processes underlying events.

Freeing of communications
Attempts are made to free up and promote communications throughout the social structure of the unit.

Flattening of authority pyramid
This happens as a result of the foregoing and is in contrast to traditional authority structures found within most psychiatric wards.

Provision of new learning experiences
Protected situations are provided, for example art classes, where patients can acquire or try out new or different ways of coping with their problems.

Role examination
This is especially relevant to the staff as it is only by constant examination and discussion that they can develop in ways appropriate to the social structure of the unit. This is also true for patients as well and both groups must balance the social requirements of the unit against their own needs.

Implicit in this is that therapeutic communities suit particular types of people. Main (1980), for instance, didn't think that schizophrenic patients could benefit from them and whilst Jones initially believed that they were useful to all, subsequent studies (Caine and Smail 1969; Copas and Whiteley 1976; Jones 1952; Whiteley 1979) suggest they are more suitable for neurotic or personality-disordered people. Whilst there have been experimental units for patients with psychotic disorders (Clark and Yeomans 1969; Cooper 1967; Pullen 1999; Wilmer 1958b), these have been exceptional and difficult to assess as such. The most dramatic example was the Villa 21 Unit, established at Shenley Hospital in 1962, whose story is related in Chapter 7. Based on the ideas of David Cooper and R.D. Laing, this unit was formed against an improbable background of existential philosophy and socialism: Cooper saw the experiment in terms of individuals struggling to find a social identity that didn't entail abandoning their 'illness' to drugs or other physical treatments. In fact, Sharp (1975) had separated out a Laing–Cooper model in which a Henderson-style community 'protects' people whilst they explore the internal meanings of their illnesses. An even better known experiment of this type was London's Kingsley Hall established by R. D. Laing also in the 1960s.

These units touched the raw nerves of conventional psychiatry because they staked a claim to its natural territory, psychosis. Whilst conventional psychiatrists were happy enough to refer (and defer) to psychotherapy those patients not seen by them as mentally *ill*, psychotic illnesses were a different matter. In time, both Villa 21 and Kingsley Hall came under intense pressures (as we shall see) and eventually closed prematurely. To the conventionalists they were akin to a running sore, constantly questioning established systems of doing things but, more so, denying the validity of the knowledge base upon which such practice was based.

Contemporary positions

By the early 1980s Hinshelwood was writing of a taxonomy of communities. In this, he was attempting to maintain the viability of the psychoanalytic versus the social model. However, the two approaches were by now clearly disproportionate, with the Cassel Hospital operating in relative isolation to a range of other forms which – in Britain at any rate – generally conformed to Jones's social model. Kennard (1983) also distinguished different types of community during the 1980s but with most of them again conforming to the social model as follows:

1. An informal and communal atmosphere

    An absence of the regimented boredom seen in larger institutions.

    Some boundaries ceasing to exist and residents and staff not being easily distinguishable. A similarity with the communalism described by Rapoport in 1960.

2. The centrality of group meetings

    These take place daily when the whole community comes together. There may be other, smaller groups. Depending on the nature of the community, the group fulfils the following functions:

    (a)   Sharing of information: a kind of 'living newspaper'.

    (b)   Building cohesion.

    (c)   Decision making becomes an open and public process. The contrast is with the 'Kafkaesque' nature of large institutions where decisions emanate from non-identifiable sources.

    (d)   A forum for personal feedback: giving and getting personal feelings and reactions.

    (c)   A vehicle whereby the community induces conformity to its goals.

3.   Sharing the work of running the community

From cooking and cleaning to decorating and administration, all therapeutic communities involve real work (as opposed to occupational therapy). Such work is important for several reasons:

(a)   It values residents as members of the community.

(b)   It encourages the acquisition of social-living skills.

(c)   It reveals problems which might remain dormant in the group work.

(d)   The moral ethic of 'good citizenship' is reflected in real work.

4.   The patient as therapist

For example, the involvement of patients in the admission process, ongoing assessments and even discharge.

Kennard's description was about the attributes endemic to most communities. There occurs a sense in which applying the Rapoport 'four principles' had become the standard formula and that this in turn bred more radical departures either, as we have seen, in terms of the kinds of patients catered for – psychotic patients at Villa 21 – or in the degree of laissez-faire in the management of affairs. In respect of the latter, Wilmer (1981) found two 'aberrant forms' which he termed 'the left' and 'the right' respectively. Communities of the left exhibited extreme permissiveness, demonstrating patients' rights and attitudes that 'often result in chaos, even anarchy'. Such an example was the perceived 'breakdown in civilised values' at Villa 21, for instance, where physical hygiene had unacceptably nose-dived and where most rules of hospital administration had been jettisoned.

Communities of the right exhibit a single ruling theory which dominates their existence, with alternative ideas or methods fiercely resented. The self-strangulation of one day hospital (Baron 1987; Hinshelwood 1980) is *the* example of the latter where the psychoanalytic interpretations of an ideologically skewed staff ran roughshod over the concerns of its patients.

Confusion

By the mid to late Eighties, therapeutic communities were clearly feeling the strain. Manning (1989) showed that there was an ideal–real gap between community aspirations and actual practice. Similarly, Bell and Ryan (1985) found that whilst staff from different communities could agree on an 'ideal form' they disagreed about the feasibility of implementing community principles in real-life settings.

In some ways, language was the problem: proliferating terminology operating at different levels of clarity widened the cracks between theory and practice. At heart, what had started out as a social therapy open to constant revision lapsed into received ideas of 'communalism' and 'democratisation'. Whilst specialist language may have been necessary so as to legitimise the new communities, the difficulty was that published work often ran ahead of practical considerations. This was true of the Rapoport (1960) study where observed difficulties were no match for a seductive terminology which was meant to characterise some of the unit's *intentions* but which many took literally.

Some other considerations

The therapeutic community can only be understood with reference to the internal and external factors by which it came about. These factors revolved around the community as an innovation as well as its movement towards wider acceptance (perhaps) and the part played by research throughout this process. The ambivalent commitment to research reflected the increasing conflict between an innovative approach and the conventional approval which it sought. In effect, innovation had to be given its 'chance' but then show results if the community was to survive. The drive for evidence ('results') came later, however, and it seems that, in its earlier stages at least, the fall off in research was less about wanting to demonstrate efficacy and more a result of a quasi-evangelical pride which saw no need for it. As Clare and Thomson (1981) discovered, evangelicalism is often the driving force behind 'new therapies'; that is, the answer has been found, no further work is required about *how* things work or what they achieve. Arthur (1973) also observed an 'anti-theoretical temperament' amongst social psychiatrists and how some therapeutic communities had acquired a defensive posture in response to external pressures.

Trauer (1984) saw this 'siege mentality' as the price to be paid by ideologically committed units: previously indisposed to research, their self-reliance

was actually an inherent weakness, their dallying with non-conformity an unconscious appeal to self-destruction.

Institutional certainties

The one sure thing about institutions is that if not constantly shaken they
gather dust. As Clark says, 'If mentally disordered people are gathered in an
institution run by doctors and nurses, that "hospital" can easily sink into
custodial nihilism with institutionalisation and often neglect, squalor and
brutality' (Clark 1999, p.37).

This is as true today as it ever was. Institutionalisation depends upon
ideology as much as on buildings, and the closure of a mental hospital does
not imply its demise. The shifting of former mental hospital wards onto the
grounds of general hospitals may actually have heightened the medicalisation
of psychiatric illnesses, and placing mental health units in 'the high street'
does not necessarily lessen restrictive approaches to care. In their book *Institutional Abuse* Stanley *et al.* (1999) comprehensively outline the dismal standards
which still prevail and it is a mistake to suppose that advances in psychopharmacology or brain imaging techniques have meant new and improved
care. The fact is, faced with a reincarnated bio-psychiatry there has never been
as much need as now for the therapeutic community impulse. For David
Clark, however, the heart has gone out of therapeutic community thinking.
He gives several reasons for this: the 'long stay' population of patients has
changed; they are not as 'able' as they once were, which is to say that pres-
ent-day patients comprise a 'hard core' of psychotic individuals who have persistently resisted most treatments. The management of care has also changed:
the entrepreneurial style of pre-1970s hospital management with its free-
wheeling superintendents is well gone; these days, bureaucracy rules.
Moreover, contemporary management favours interventions whose outcomes
are quantitatively measurable. Psychiatry is now saddled with the political
short straw of managing 'care in the community' with ever-diminishing funds
and ability to provide shelter only for those seen as dangerous. Hence, the
rising star of forensic psychiatry which may stem from concerns about personality disordered people in the community. This is the group for whom therapeutic communities have always seemed best suited and, predictably, some of
the forensic units now declared themselves 'therapeutic communities'. The
Reed Committee, charged with reviewing services for mentally disordered
offenders, stated that: 'more specialist units comparable to the Henderson
Hospital should be developed' (Reed Committee 1994, p.43).

This led to the development of two forensic units – one in the Midlands and one in the north-east of England – based on the Henderson Model and, over time, others followed although the present writer (Clarke 1999) demonstrated that in these instances the divergence between public claims and actual practice was very wide.

The present

In our own time, communities have – like everyone else – looked to 'the community' as the matrix within which to operate. The Cassel, for instance, has been developing community outreach programmes since 1995 (Pringle and Chiesa 2001). Tucker (2000) has similarly outlined a therapeutic community approach to care in the community and has described Community Housing and Therapy (CHT) which operates six therapeutic communities for severely mentally ill and homeless people. It remains to be seen how these community-based operations will develop: recall that whilst many of the first communities emerged within existing hospitals, this conferred advantages in that they could reflect (hermit-like) on how the wider society might be implicated in their psychological distress. In effect, removal from the wider society led to a paradoxical capability to 're-represent' oneself in society, allowing discussion from the vantage point of safety and distance. In this, the communities had something in common with the theatre: constructed realities which are not literal but which inform perception by removing some of the barriers which close down imagination and expression.

There is – tentatively – a sense in which therapeutic communities are back. At least the self-doubt which descended in the 1980s is lifting. Even Rapoport's four principles continue to shape current therapeutic community writings (Haigh 1999), although most contemporary writers also point to the continuing need to convince outside agencies – such as government funders – of their remedial value: this need will be discussed further in Chapter 8.

The current stance

In an important paper, Lindsay (1982), a former Henderson resident, acknowledged the four principles in action but also observed their dissolution if problems required a 'traditional' – hierarchical – solution. Maxwell Jones (1980) knew this, saying that at times of crises, an open system may have to reintroduce controls involving, for instance, temporary authoritarian regimes. Such ideas, having once operated in relatively covert fashion are now a pivotal component of a 'rejuvenated' Henderson approach comprising more conventional elements of practice. Lees *et al.* (1999), for instance, designate effectiveness, replication and evidence-based thinking as major requirements for contemporary community practice. Communities continue to introduce themselves to residents as structures which recognise the needs and wants (and deficiencies) of its members. But now, if residents break that structure they can be considered to have discharged themselves and must apply for reinstatement. Several questions arise from this. Can the structure be altered? For example, can negotiation of the form of the structure be part of the process of reinstatement? How and by whom did this structure come about? Is it a fore-ordained, external and immutable framework? Or is it a system in tension: dynamic, unpredictable, creative? Professor Kathleen Jones (1972) once commented on what she saw as the naivety of therapeutic communities, but this is not something she could repeat with conviction today. Actually, Professor Jones agrees that the first communities significantly influenced mental hospitals: in many ways, they represented the best that practical psychiatry could do for institutionalised patients.

However, the problems of the Fifties and Sixties were obvious. It was clear what needed to be done and, at a time of minimal accountability within the NHS, the reformers got on with the job. All that is changed: communities now have to account more explicitly for the effects of their interventions whilst simultaneously trying to retain the philosophical principles which give them their distinctiveness. However, it is a distinction that does not lend itself to interventions which yield to statistical review. What is required are outcome evaluations which avoid undue emphasis on introspection whilst accentuating interventions and outcomes that can be communicated effectively. It is not semantic forms of research which provoke criticism as much as their perceived failure to communicate data concisely. That perception has festered for years due to the heterogeneity of community practices preventing concerted responses to criticisms and questions. An easy solution would be to call for an organised programme of research with terms and conditions agreed – perhaps by an international convention. However, heterogeneity – of philosophy, principles, practice – runs deep: historically, communities have *celebrated* diversity. Therefore, trying to force agreements as to what principles might mean in practice would probably lead to discord.

References

Abroms, G.M. (1969) 'Defining milieu therapy.' *Archives of General Psychiatry 21*, 553–560.

Arthur, R.J. (1973) 'Social psychiatry: an overview.' *American Journal of Psychiatry 130*, 841–849.

Baron, C. (1987) *Asylum into Anarchy*. London: Free Association Books.

Barton, R. (1957) *Institutional Neurosis*. Bristol: John Wright and Sons Ltd.

Belknap, I. (1956) *Human Problems of a State Mental Hospital*. New York: McGraw-Hill.

Bell, M.D. and Ryan, E.R. (1985) 'Where can therapeutic community ideals be realised? An examination of three treatment environments.' *Hospital and Community Psychiatry 36*, 1286–1291.

Bickford, J.A.R. (1958) 'Shadow and substance: some changes in the mental hospital.' *Lancet* (22 February), 423–424.

Bion, W. (1961) *Experiences in Groups*. London: Tavistock Publications.

Caine, T.M. and Smail, D.J. (1969) *The Treatment of Mental Illness: Science, Faith and the Therapeutic Personality*. London: University of London Press.

Carstairs, G.M. and Heron, A. (1957) 'The social environment of mental hospital patients: a measure of staff attitudes.' In M. Greenblat, D.J. Levinson and R.N. Williams (eds) *The Patient and the Mental Hospital*. Glencoe: The Free Press.

Caudill, W. (1958) *The Psychiatric Hospital as a Small Society*. Cambridge: Harvard University Press.

Clare, A. and Thomson, S. (1981) *Let's Talk About Me*. London: BBC Publications.

Clark, A.W. and Yeomans, N.T. (1969) *Fraser House Theory, Practice and Evaluation of a Therapeutic Community*. New York: Springer-Verlag.

Clark, D.H. (1958) 'Administrative therapy: its clinical importance in the mental hospital.' *Lancet i*, 805–808.

Clark, D.H. (1964) *Administrative Therapy*. London: Tavistock.

Clark, D.H. (1965) 'The therapeutic community concept, practice and future.' *British Journal of Psychiatry 11*, 1, 947–954.

Clark, D. (1999) 'Social psychiatry: the therapeutic community approach.' In P. Campling and R. Haigh (eds) *Therapeutic Communities, Past, Present and Future*. London: Jessica Kingsley Publishers.

Clarke, L. (1999) *Challenging Ideas in Psychiatric Nursing*. London: Routledge.

Cooper, D. (1967) *Psychiatry and Anti-psychiatry*. London: Paladin.

Copas, J.B. and Whiteley, S. (1976) 'Predicting success in the treatment of psychopaths.' *British Journal of Psychiatry 129*, 388–392.

Crockett, R.W. (1960) 'Doctor, administrator and the therapeutic community.' *Lancet ii*, 359–363.

Crockett, R.W. (1978) 'Community time structure.' *Association of Therapeutic Communities Bulletin 25*, 12–17.

Denber, H.C.B. (1960) *Research Conference on Therapeutic Community*. Springfield, Chicago: C.H. Thomas.

Dietrich, G. (1976) 'Nurses in the therapeutic community.' *Journal of Advanced Nursing 1*, 139–154.

Dunham, H.W. and Weinberg, S.K. (1960) *The Culture of the State Mental Hospital*. Detroit: Wayne State University Press.

Foulkes, S.H. (1964) *Therapeutic Group Analysis*. London: George Allen and Unwin Ltd.

Garnett, M.H. and Schlunke, J.M. (1984) 'The couple in a small therapeutic community.' *International Journal of Therapeutic Communities 5*, 4.

Greenblat, M., Levinson, D.J. and Williams, R.N. (1957) *The Patient and the Mental Hospital*. Glencoe: Free Press.

Haigh, R. (1999) 'The quintessence of a therapeutic community.' In P. Campling and R. Haigh (eds) *Therapeutic Communities: Past, Present and Future*. London: Jessica Kingsley Publishers.

Hinshelwood, R.D. (1980) 'The seeds of disaster.' *International Journal of Therapeutic Communities 1*, 3.

Hinshelwood, R.D. (1999) 'Psychoanalytic origins and today's work.' In P. Campling and R. Haigh (eds) *Therapeutic Communities: Past, Present and Future.* London: Jessica Kingsley Publishers.

Jansen, E. (1980) 'Introduction.' In E. Jansen (ed) *The Therapeutic Community.* London: Croom Helm.

Jones, K. (1972) *A History of the Mental Health Services.* London: Routledge and Kegan Paul.

Jones, M. (1952) *Social Psychiatry.* London: Routledge and Kegan Paul.

Jones, M. (1953) *The Therapeutic Community: A New Treatment Method in Psychiatry.* New York: Basic Books.

Jones, M. (1968) *Social Psychiatry in Practice.* Harmondsworth: Penguin Books.

Jones, M. (1980) 'Will therapeutic communities survive and grow?' *International Journal of Therapeutic Communities 1*, 2.

Kennard, D. (1979) Limiting factors: the setting, the staff, the patients. In R.D. Hinshelwood and N.P. Manning (eds) *Therapeutic Communities: Reflections and Progress.* London: Routledge and Kegan Paul.

Kennard, D. (1983) *An Introduction to Therapeutic Communities.* London: Routledge and Kegan Paul.

Lees, J., Manning, N. and Rawlings, B. (1999) *Therapeutic Community Effectiveness.* York: NHS Centre for Reviews and Dissemination, University of York.

Lindsay, M. (1982) 'A critical view of the validity of the therapeutic community.' *Nursing Times, Occasional Papers 78*, 27, 105–107.

Main, T. (1946) 'The hospital as a therapeutic community.' *Bulletin of the Menninger Clinic 10*, 66–70.

Main, T. (1980) 'Some basic concepts in therapeutic community work.' In E. Jansen (ed) *The Therapeutic Community.* London: Croom Helm.

Manning, N.P. (1979) 'The politics of survival: the role of research in the therapeutic community.' In R.D. Hinshelwood and N.P. Manning (eds) *Therapeutic Communities: Reflections and Progress.* London: Routledge and Kegan Paul.

Manning, N.P. (1989) *The Therapeutic Community Movement: Charisma and Routinisation.* London: Routledge.

Maratos, J. and Kennedy, M.J. (1974) 'Evaluation of ward group meetings in a psychiatric unit of a general hospital.' *British Journal of Psychiatry 125*, 479–482.

Marohn, R.C. (1970) 'The therapeutic milieu as an open system.' *Archives of General Psychiatry 22*, 360–364.

Martin, D.V. (1955) 'Institutionalisation.' *Lancet ii*, 1188–1190.

Martin, J.P. (1984) *Hospitals in Trouble.* Oxford: Basic Blackwell.

Moos, R. (1974) *Evaluating Treatment Environments: A Social Ecological Approach.* New York: Wiley, New York.

Price, R.H. and Moos, R.H. (1975) 'Towards a taxonomy of inpatient treatment environments.' *Journal of Abnormal Psychology 84*, 181–188.

Pringle, P. and Chiesa, M. (2001) 'From the therapeutic community to the community: developing an outreach psychosocial nursing service for severe personality disorders.' *Therapeutic Communities 22*, 3, 215–232.

Pullen, G. (1999) 'Schizophrenia: hospital communities for the severely disturbed.' In P. Campling and R. Haigh (eds) *Therapeutic Communities: Past, Present and Future.* London: Jessica Kingsley Publishers.

Ramon, S. (1985) *Psychiatry in Britain: Meaning and Policy.* London: Croom Helm.

Rapoport, R.N. (1960) *Community as Doctor: New Perspectives on a Therapeutic Community.* London: Tavistock.

Reed Committee (1994) *Report of the Department of Health and Home Office Working Group on Psychopathic Disorder.* London: Department of Health and Home Office (Chairman, Dr John Reed).

Rees, T.P. (1957) 'Back to moral treatment and community care.' *Journal of Mental Science 103*, 303–313.

Rossi, J.J. and Filstead, W.J. (1973) 'Therapeutic milieu: therapeutic community, and milieu therapy: some conceptual and definitional distinctions.' In J.J. Rossi and W.J. Filstead (eds) *The Therapeutic Community: a Sourcebook of Readings.* New York: Behavioural Publications.

Sharp, V. (1975) *Social Control in the Therapeutic Community.* Lexington House, MA: Saxon Books.

Shoenberg, E. (1980) 'Therapeutic communities: the ideal, the real and the possible.' In E. Jansen (ed) *The Therapeutic Community.* London: Croom Helm.

Stanley, N., Manthorpe, J. and Penhale, B. (1999) *Institutional Abuse: Perspective Across the Life Course.* London: Routledge.

Stanton, A.H. and Schwartz, M.S. (1954) *The Mental Hospital.* New York: Basic Books.

Stubbledine, J. (1960) 'The therapeutic community: a further formulation.' *Mental Hospitals 11*, 16–18.

Towell, D. (1975) *Understanding Psychiatric Nursing.* London: RCN Publications.

Trauer, T. (1979) 'The relationship between large group meetings and patients' estimates of ward tension.' *British Journal of Medical Psychology 52*, 205–213.

Trauer, T. (1980) 'Correlates of patient participation in the large group meetings of a therapeutic community.' *British Journal of Medical Psychology 53*, 109–166.

Trauer, T. (1984) 'The current status of the therapeutic community.' *British Journal of Medical Psychology 57*, 71–79.

Tucker, S. (2000) 'Introduction: why we need a therapeutic community approach to care in the community.' In S. Tucker (ed) *A Therapeutic Community Approach to care in the Community.* London: Jessica Kingsley Publishers.

Whiteley, S. (1979) 'Progress and reflection.' In R.D. Hinshelwood and N.P. Manning (eds) *Therapeutic Communities: Reflections and Progress.* London: Routledge and Kegan Paul.

Whiteley, S. (1990) 'Obituary. Professor Maxwell Jones: the psychiatrist as social ecologist.' *The Guardian* 20 August.

Wilmer, H.A. (1958a) 'Towards a definition of therapeutic community.' *American Journal of Psychiatry 114*, 828–834.

Wilmer, H.A. (1958b) *Social Psychiatry in Action: A Therapeutic Community.* Illinois: C.C. Thomas.

Wilmer, H.A. (1981) 'Defining and understanding the therapeutic community.' *Hospital and Community Psychiatry 32*, 2, 95–99.

World Health Organisation (1953) *Expert Committee on Mental Health, 3rd Report.* Geneva: WHO.

Zeitlyn, B.B. (1967) 'The therapeutic community: fact or fantasy?' *British Journal of Psychiatry 1*, 13, 1083–1086.

CHAPTER 6

R.D. Laing and Divided Selves

It is only when one is able to gather from the individual himself the history of his self, and not what a psychiatric history in these circumstances usually is, the history of the false-self system, that his psychosis becomes explicable.

R.D. Laing (1960)

Abiding Presence

The first thing that struck me about him was the Glasgow hardman's accent, the wreathed face, what Jeff Nutall called the 'ah'm-fucken-taillen-ye' expression. Ronnie Laing was someone whose shoes you wouldn't spit on in a hurry. And this was a psychiatrist: more, a philosopher manqué mouthing strange things about madness and medicalisation. 'What kind of doctor is this?', I asked one of my tutors. 'I'll tell you what kind', he replied, 'he's a madman, pay him no heed, he's a passing fancy'.

And in an awful way, the last bit came true. 'Did you used to be R.D. Laing?' an old woman asked him towards the end of the 1980s. Indeed, throughout the Eighties, reports of Ronnie's demise were as common as they were comical. To most psychiatric practitioners, he had, by this time, become 'an interesting, extremely idiosyncratic, product of 1960s psychedelic culture, but best consigned to history and, of course, quite mad' (Davidson 1998, p.64). And in the fullness of time, a compilation by the *Sunday Times* (1999) of the '100 Greatest Scots' (which included Lulu and Annie Lennox) excluded him.

Person

From the moment of conception Ronald Laing was an embarrassment. The sexual derivation of her swollen womb had made his mother cover it up with a large overcoat. Indeed, as she neither sought him in life nor did she want him in death: she forbade him to attend her funeral but he went anyway and wept profusely. She would have loathed such a public display: what his fellow psychoanalysts made of it is anybody's guess. An only child, Laing was born into the lower middle-class gentility of Govanahill, Glasgow, on 7 October 1927 and was buried there 62 years later, having died of a heart attack playing tennis in, of all places, St Tropez. Emotionally adrift from an early age, he never got on with his mother: so much so that his son Adrian recalls (Laing 1994) how, even in middle age, Laing's visits to her were excruciatingly uncomfortable. She *was* strange. Over-concerned with social status, she sent Ronnie to 'the right school' and saw to it that he did not mix with riffraff (Laing 1994, p.22). However, it must have been a perversity of some kind which made her give away his best-loved toys. In an age not fashionable for such things, she would tell the five-year-old Laing that there was no Santa Claus: ontological insecurity came early for Ronnie. Of course it is not just a question of blame, and making connections between 'abusive' parenting and psychiatric strife in later life is nowadays an over-ripe activity. The fact is that none of us escape the oedipal jive. Laing knew full well the effects of his upbringing on his later beliefs. Having failed all of his medical examinations first time around, he recalled some years later, 'Well, there was one class in medical school that I came out at the top of my year, skin diseases' (Mullan 1995, p.64). It's hardly a surprise – he was, after all, a psychoanalyst – that he saw a connection between this particular 'success' and his martyrdom to eczema.

Laing was to remain an outsider, always; to his early families; certainly to psychoanalysis (about which he was always ambivalent); to the medical establishment, which forced him off its register. Eventually, he would sell himself short with attempt after attempt to retain the fame that had sucked him dry of ideas and, after a long struggle, life. Matters were not helped by (alcohol-fuelled) public posturing as well as, not infrequently, fisticuffs. Appearing on Irish television – drunk – discussion about his life or work was impossible, and his host, Gay Byrne, plainly annoyed, made his feelings known there and then. Adrian Laing described this as a 'Viking phase' in his father's life, an intoxicated scramble to forge a new identity. Provocatively, Laing thought it funny that the Irish should object to his drunkenness and was delighted when, returning to England, he was offered whiskey whilst still on the Dublin tarmac and his co-passengers cheered. Watching his television performance, his first wife, Anne Hearn Laing, likened her former husband to 'a caged animal'. But how foolish of him to suppose that he could appear drunk in an Irish setting and *not* be challenged over it, and this his host duly did. Given another chance to argue his position, he characteristically threw it away and he was never able to say why, other than to mutter occasionally about the terrors of 'Celtic involutional melancholia' (Clare 1996).

After qualifying

After qualifying as a doctor in 1951, R.D. Laing chose psychiatry as his speciality. Initially, he followed the typical career path of junior hospital posts, doctor's rounds, crowded back wards and routine drug prescribing. However, an attachment to philosophical inquiry as well as a serious commitment to the Hippocratic Oath led him to reconsider the nature of doctor–patient relationships, as well as to re-evaluate schizophrenia less as an illness and more as 'another way of being human' (Jenner *et al.* 1993). In 1960, his book *The Divided Self* challenged many of the ideas which underpinned psychiatry as a medical speciality. Written during the late 1950s, the genesis of this book lay in the post-war chronic wards of GarthNaval Hospital in Glasgow. Turned down by many publishers it was eventually printed by Tavistock Publications and quickly became a best seller. Its dramatic opening comprised an 'unmasking' of the inadequacies of Kraepelian diagnosis as well as a brilliant portrayal of schizophrenia as something altogether more complex and mysterious. Laing could make conventional psychiatric practice *sound* hilarious – one of a (very small) number of attributes he shares with Thomas Szasz. This was a book which served notice that psychiatric theory was about to be undermined and in a manner which brooked little contradiction. It criticised much of 'clinical psychiatry' and did so with the consummate ease and competency of true scholarship. In addition, the book fell well within the confines of orthodoxy: there was nothing flippant about it, nothing aggrandising or forced.

This is important because Laing's analyst, Charles Rycroft, believed that his eventual downfall resulted from straying from the conventional fold. Anthony Storr (1996) agreed, suggesting that it was his role as prophet, his world-wide fame, which inflated his ego and ultimately corrupted him. Whatever the reasons, Laing's work increasingly found refuge outside mainstream psychiatry, such that by the 1970s he had acquired the persona of a gangster: gangster in a Celtic sense of troublemaker and spoiler; increasingly disgruntled unless disgruntling others, alternately self-pitying and destructive. Laing's resistance to 'the conformity of psychiatric ideas' might have seemed more credible had he found a way of fixing himself within the medical establishment and their way of doing things. But he couldn't content himself with producing subdued, scholarly works or with practising conventional psychiatry or psychoanalysis. His writing progressively reflected a radical 'notoriety', less in the sense – comparable to Thomas Szasz let's say – of sustaining challenging ideas, but more in the production of disconnected, wild, or occasionally trivial compositions. It seems such a pity when one considers the innovative brilliance of his first book *The Divided Self.* One hesitates to exaggerate its influence but, for some, it was a breathtaking (yet plausible) departure from conventional medical thinking, advancing as it did the notion that how schizophrenics *experienced and reported* their 'illness' was important. According to Robert Young (1966), Laing 'surely succeeds in making one feel, yes it must be like that to be mad': the contention was that what professionals call delusions actually make sense within the terms of reference of the individual experiencing them. In this book, Laing abandoned psychoanalysis in favour of existentialism which in turn allowed him to construct the theory that the self 'divides' in favour of itself, where the individual evolves an alternative (fantasy) world which functions to protect 'the self' from outside forces. It was this blending of existentialism into a psychological tract on schizophrenia which was so exhilarating. Like Ayer's *Language, Truth and Logic*, *The Divided Self* corralled ideas and made them seem legitimate in their time and place. It was internally consistent and it derived much of its power from its roots in conventional psychiatry. Appalled that Colin Wilson had got the jump on him with *The Outsider*, Laing was equally incensed that London seemed full of 'angry young men' and he wasn't one of them. In his youth he had set the cut-off point at which he would find fame at age 30. By the 1960s he was desperate it might never happen. He need not have worried. By the late 1960s, early 1970s, he was a world-wide celebrity. In England he frequented TV chat shows; Ken Loach (1971) directed a feature film, *Family Life*, based on his ideas; and in America, *Life* magazine had him on its front cover under the banner 'Philosopher of Madness'. Did he anticipate any of this? It becomes difficult to know. When *The Divided Self* appeared, the psychiatric establishment looked on it as little more than an interesting aside, a welcome interlude at conferences and seminars, perhaps, but not germane to everyday practice. In later years, Laing would bitterly comment, 'You think I've cut into the conscience of everyone Martin Roth teaches? My work has not made the slightest difference – in fact it has only entrenched them' (Mullan 1995, p.378). Yet he may well have imagined the public fame that would come his way: the likelihood is that he traded professional standing for the fame.

Anti-psychiatry

Against his wishes, Laing was called an 'anti-psychiatrist' (by David Cooper 1968), partly because it was supposed that he had denied that schizophrenia existed or, if it did, that its victims either inhabited a higher spiritual plane or were an oppressed minority within materialist (capitalist) systems. In fact, Laing said none of these things. Rather did he suggest that schizophrenia merited the same regard accorded to any mental state, and that merely to approach it as an illness was to demean its significance. In *The Divided Self* he demonstrated how the diagnostic process added to the patient's problems by defining behaviour as 'illness', behaviour which, said Laing, was just as explicable in terms of the social life of the patient. On the question of schizophrenia being *caused* by families, the argument, actually, was that the sometimes bizarre and apparently meaningless aspects of schizophrenia may be more meaningfully understood in the context of how families are experienced.

Relationships with his own patients were, however, idiosyncratic (Reed 1974) and in the twilight of his career, charges brought against him concerning his intoxication – later withdrawn – led to his 'retirement' from the medical register. By the late Seventies he was drinking very heavily (often with attendant anti-social behaviour) and his reputation had all but expired. Today, his ideas are no longer fashionable (albeit showing signs of revival: witness a recent spate of biographies by Burston 1996, 2000; Clay 1997; Kotowicz 1997; Laing 1994; Mullan 1995).

Conventional psychiatry, which reeled under the onslaught of his 1960s radicalism, survived his anti-psychiatric critique, even vanquished it. But whilst Laingian thinking did not dislodge medical perspectives it did influence them a lot. Laing made it uncomfortable for anyone wanting to treat 'mental illnesses' as though these were objective entities unencumbered by subjective experience. Following him, it became less easy to dismiss the experiences of schizophrenic patients as a product of deranged brains, or to negate the beliefs of schizophrenic patients as thought disorders, hallucinations or delusions.

Historical contexts

Laingian psychiatry was but one of a batch of radical departures which hindsight has designated the counterculture of the 1960s. Its emergence can be earmarked by the reintroduction of the word 'madness' into psychiatric terminology. Some philosopher/historians of the period, for example Foucault (1971) and Scull (1979) began to explicate history in terms of how western society had 'subdued madness', usually as a means towards its own social, especially economic ends. It was Laing, in fact, who had revitalised the word 'madman' (in *The Divided Self*) partly as a dramatic device but also so as to broaden ongoing concepts of mental illness. Apart from a book by Henry Yellowlees (1953) and another by John Curtance (1951), 'madness' had ceased to have psycho-linguistic currency for over 30 years, indeed until

Laing's first book. (Intriguingly, the title of Curtance's book *Wisdom, Madness and Folly* became the title of Laing's autobiography.)

The 1960s was (supposedly) the era of free love, anti-war, stimulant drugs, long-hair and Woodstock, challenges to established norms being driven by artists, intellectuals, students and, in France, at any rate, by the proletariat. In Great Britain, student unrest was never as boisterous as on the continent and only small numbers embraced the various protest movements that have come to symbolise the period. In many respects 'the Swinging Sixties' is a never-never land concocted by social pundits and wishful thinkers; as we explored in Chapter 1, it was a more contradictory period than many imagine.

Yet something happened, some dislocation in the way that people thought about their lives, society, their roles in society. Women's groups, especially, began to produce feminist critiques of history and society. Regrettably, such activities were the prerogative of a few, for despite trying to connect with working-class women, the latter opposed 'feminisation' resolutely. Although the 1960s witnessed legislative changes in abortion, fair pay and divorce, the constraints of economic inequality and patriarchal dominion within families continued to define most women's lives.

> Denied by their education any real opportunity to understand their world outside the constraints and identities of their roles as wives, mothers, workers or school girls, women coped with change within the resources of their experience and power. (Williamson 1990, p.188)

In this context the predominance of female clients within Laingian therapy might suggest radical psychiatry's willingness to address a neglected group: equally, however, it could represent the (more devious) side of an otherwise oppressive coin.

Periods of history

In the Preface Arthur Marwick (1998) reflected on the vagaries of 'periodisation', chopping the past into (more readable) eras and decades. Part of the problem of historic 'periods', such as 'the Sixties', is that they may not be definitive of the events they are meant to represent since, often, the events themselves irritatingly contradict the periods concerned. It's a strange thought, really, that Sir William Sargant's autobiography was published seven years *after The Divided Self.* Sargant, doyen of establishment psychiatry, arch exponent of physical treatments, called his book *The Unquiet Mind: The Autobiography of a Physician in Psychological Medicine* (1967). He once told Laing –

following a television appearance where Laing sought to demystify some aspects of psychiatry – that he (Laing) was a doctor and so should not 'speak like that in front of the children' (Mullan 1995, p.256). It was during this period that psychiatrists were struggling to entrench their discipline within the medical fraternity, and efforts were underway to create a Royal College of Psychiatrists (established in 1971) and move psychiatric wards out of the old mental hospitals and onto the grounds of general hospitals. How ironic that the anti-psychiatric radicals – who have come to characterise 1960s psychiatry – actually ran parallel to an evolving conventionalism within the profession overall. As the Sixties progressed, Laing's activities began to diversify and, for example, he developed an interest in eastern philosophy and meditation. How some of his conservative colleagues must have loathed the spectacle of him posing in a loincloth whilst standing on his head, a dose of eastern mysticism aimed at the heart of scientism and, as he saw it, western medical arrogance.

Sixties sellers

As well as *The Divided Self,* Ervin Goffman's *Asylums* (1968) and Ken Kesey's *One Flew Over the Cuckoo's Nest* (1963) also became best sellers. Products of their authors' experiences, in different ways these books sought to convey the potential terrors of institutional psychiatry. In Kesey's case, even 'good' practices like group therapy might not be what they seemed, and Nurse Ratched just about personified psychiatric malevolence.

But it was Joseph Heller's *Catch 22* (1962) which captured the contradictions and paradoxes of 'normal' versus 'abnormal' behaviour. In this novel, Yossarian, a fighter pilot, wants to prolong his life and so requests that he be relieved of flying extra bombing missions on grounds of being crazy. The doctor says that he *can* be relieved but first he must request it. Yossarian's predicament mirrors patients who voluntarily enter psychiatric hospitals but when subsequently wanting to leave are prevented from doing so by the imposition of a legal 'holding power'. In other words: I was sane to want to come here but insane if I want to go. Laing frequently drew attention to the odd contradictions that psychiatry brings to bear on everyday living. For instance, he would describe how his daughter was committed to an institution having been found kneeling outside a church in pouring rain. Apart from the disreputable fact of her forced detention it was all the more inexplicable, he insisted, because had she been kneeling *inside* the church she might well have been treated differently.

Generally, at this time, psychiatric dissidents regarded physical treatments such as drugs or electricity as anathema because they signified the destruction of individual consciousness. Truth to tell, if one word characterised the counterculture of the Sixties and Seventies it was consciousness (in all its forms): alternative, raised, expanding, restricting, imploding, exploding, psychedelic, schizoid. Questions such as 'what does it mean to be free?' and, 'How do I become free?' preoccupied radical/juvenile thought. Bob Dylan said that the answers were 'Blowing in the Wind' which seemed to suggest that there *were* no answers, or that what had till then worked as answers were no longer enough. The key thing to do now was to opt out. Timothy Leary's call to 'tune in and drop out' fell on no end of willing ears and as the Sixties proceeded, student revolt and worker unrest (in France) momentarily threatened the French government. Although student unrest was also afoot in England, its radical edge found little sympathy amongst workers and, in any event, the British genius for muffling dissent came to the fore, with the lowering of the voting age to 18 just prior to the 1970 general election.

In general, the basics to which future generations would want to go back were falling one by one. There were revisions of the law pertaining to divorce, abortion, homosexuality and criminality. The consequences of these changes are still unravelling and with much debate as to whether they represent progressive or retrogressive watersheds. For our purposes, it is the link between social/legal changes and the counterculture rhetoric of 'the Sixties', particularly in psychiatry, which is at issue. It is curious that the philosophical, academic, artistic concerns which Laing spearheaded seemed unconnected to developments in public policy. Questioned about this, he responded:

> There's a lot of the way our society works which I haven't really been able to see my way through into any post neo-Marxist unified theory of a systematic order of society like that. If I could have developed something like that I would be very glad to, who wouldn't? I hadn't either the talent, the genius, the vision to see my way through that. (in Mullan 1995, p.343)

In Peter Sedgwick's view, whilst Laing appeared to present a social (psychiatric) perspective, he was simply indulging in fashionable New Left chic. In addition, says Sedgwick, this lack of a social framework permitted Laing to espouse a mystical theory of schizophrenia as 'a rationale for non-intervention in a schizophrenic's delusions' (Sedgwick 1982, p.100), the experience of which resulted (supposedly in Laing's view) in the schizophrenic being 'shunted off into a garbage heap for incineration by sanitary technicians' (Sedgwick 1982, p.100). The violence of the last sentence reflects Sedgwick's determination to bring in a guilty verdict on Laing who never used language like this. Of course, the conceptual, political standing of Laing's writing can be criticised: he himself needed no reminding of its inconsistencies and contradictions. But his work did re-awaken interest in schizophrenia as worthy of philosophical inquiry, as well as add to concerns about the manner in which mental patients were being treated. That is surely a credit not easily set aside.

Rebel guru

As the Seventies proceeded, Laing's ascension to guru status eroded his place within psychiatry. 'After Freud and Jung, now comes R.D. Laing, Pop-shrink, rebel, yogi, philosopher king, latest re-incarnation of Aescu-lapius...' (Mezan 1972). However, guru status doesn't come easy. In Laing's case it came in two stages. The first involved the publication of *Sanity, Madness and the Family* (Laing and Esterson 1970) wherein (despite dogged denials) 'the family' was clearly implicated in the genesis of schizophrenia. The second stage was marked by his book *The Politics of Experience and the Bird of Paradise* (1967), which caught the Sixties air of half-baked estrangement beautifully, weaving its way in and out of a freedom/oppression circuit with the assuredness of a prestidigitator. It sold in prodigious quantities and Laing noted, self-approvingly, how people constantly approached him saying how much it had changed their lives. However – and it's a big however – its *schizophrenia is a voyage* chapter would return forever and a day to haunt him. For whatever schizophrenia might be, it caused distress: it ravaged lives; it was here on earth, not in the stars, and Laing made a big mistake in saying that it was. All who knew him agree that he genuinely liked psychotic people, their company; that (like Bierer: see Chapter 3) he was always happily animated in their presence. That said, he surrendered his objectivity about schizophrenia and for little else other than that the times required it and he lacked the intellectual steadfastness to ride above his reverential audience.

The alternative consciousness

As time passed, he embraced roles which belittled him. He became an 'agony aunt', a 'recording artist', a 'poet', some say a fool. Agonisingly, his books descended to triviality and iconoclasm, his 'poetry' especially drew ascerbic dissension. Looking back, I guess you might say he was the archetypal postmodernist, resolutely committed to the ridiculous and the sublime in equal measure, aware more than most of the futility of 'final truths'. This may be too kind though. Laing had a mischievous streak – on film, he often *looks* mischievous – and he loved playing to the galleries. However, conference grandstanding could wear a bit thin and his son recalls his father's wearying participation in endless 'new age' therapy sessions and all for the sake of 'making a few bob'. Everything got tougher as the years went by.

Although acutely aware of his mounting vulnerability as a significant intellectual, try as he might he could never solve the problem of producing 'another major book', a work which would spring *The Divided Self* from the purgatory of 'single good idea'. Eventually he contented himself with past glories, trundling out anecdotes and indulging in a knife-edge act of intellectual debate whilst (often) drunk and despairingly incoherent.

Mad to be normal

Laing despised authority, holding back even within his psychoanalysis. (His analyst, Charles Rycroft, has not violated the confidentiality of this protracted event – and, in our age of 'tell all' diaries and revealing memoirs, this is to his credit). It is difficult to fathom why Laing trained as an analyst for he never showed any commitment to its principles (see Clay 1997, pp.65–66). He refused to practise classical psychoanalysis (in fairness does anybody?) and would remain 'his own man' within the different treatment milieus in which he worked. However, idiosyncratic approaches to patients led to accusations of dilettantism (and worse) and his last years were spent trying to refute these. In particular, he vehemently rejected Elaine Showalter's accusation that he had used Mary Barnes, that Barnes's so-called schizophrenic 'voyage' had enabled him to act out heroic fantasies of male rescue and so forth. Whilst Laing's rebuttal (see Mullan 1995, pp.323–325) of this is persuasive, his manner of dealing with the case of Anna (Reed 1974) is more problematic. In part, this is because Reed's allegations are directed at Laingian therapy and not just at the man himself. That said, Laing had had little to do with Anna – who committed suicide – other than one or two encounters with both her and David Reed, her husband. According to Reed, these encounters, one a chance meeting in a London street and the other a visit to Anna's flat, depict a nonchalant Laing content to stand back and watch the patient 'progress' through her psychotic journey or 'trip'. Kotowicz (1997) quotes Claridge on this point:

> It is not – for all its insights and intellectual brilliance – Laing's *The Divided Self* that makes the greater impact; rather is it David Reed's *Anna*, the tragic story of an individual schizophrenic who was persuaded by a Laingian doctor to face up to her madness without drugs, and whose slow, painful

> death from self-inflicted burns symbolises in the most awful way the end of
> an era in psychiatry. (Claridge 1990, p.157)

Apart from the fact that the issue was electric treatment and not drugs it hardly
surprises that the kind of articulate people who became Laing's patients would
write up their experiences with him. Whereas, as an annoyed Laing pointed
out, in-patient and out-patient departments across the land have had frequent
suicides and not a word about it. Why blacken his name by recalling the
suicide of a single patient whom he had only met twice? Apparently suffering
from schizophrenia, Anna rejected conventional psychiatry and sought out
Laing who referred her to one of his disciples, Dr Roy Landis. Denied electric
treatment (Laing said, it would 'shock the psychosis back into her' (Reed
1974, p.55)) from which she had benefited in the past, she failed to make
progress and took her life. The case *does* stand in stark contrast to the intellectual bravura of Laingian psychiatry and whilst Laing's biographers eulogise
the bravura and the brilliance, they never mention Anna. But although the
case does not define who he was, personally or professionally, it does raise
issues in respect of Laingian therapy and women patients.

Women

To some extent, Laing's psychology reinforced fatuous notions of maternal responsibility for mental illness. However, allegations of superman fantasies and
casualness (in respect of female patients) must be seen in a psychiatric context
that has consistently treated women as second class. Laing was no different
from others of his generation and was better than some. In an account of psychology and women, Miller states, 'To be treated like an object is to be threatened with psychological annihilation. It is a truly dreadful experience. Several
writers have popularised the role it plays in psychological writings, for
example, R.D. Laing' (Miller 1988, p.59).

Laing's accounts of the back wards of GarthNavel Hospital, where he
began, display his affinity with chronic female patients which verges on the
maternal and even Showalter (1985, p.222) concedes that he exposed many
of the assumptions about female dependence, passivity, chastity, dutifulness,
obedience which psychiatry emphasised.

There is no question that Laing's domain was an all male affair. Take the
infamous July 1967 Dialectics of Liberation Conference at the Roundhouse.
Although ostensibly about social justice, a striking feature of the speakers'
line-up was the absence of women! Similarly, the core group of therapists at
Kingsley Hall were called 'the brothers' and women were either patients or

elevated to the symbolic safety zone of 'ethereal child' or 'cosmic mother'. As noted, its most famous patient, Mary Barnes, co-wrote a book with her therapist (Barnes and Berke 1971). But, in general, women played a small part in the ownership or application of new psychiatric ideas. And this is probably true across the board: on joining the staff at Winterbourne therapeutic community Jane Knowles recalls:

> You did not need to be a feminist with a natural allergy to patriarchy to see the innate dangers of charismatic and socially powerful male figures being in such a position of authority with some of the most personality damaged women and men in Berkshire. (Knowles 2001, p.273)

Mothers and sons

When I began working in mental hospitals in the 1970s I was apprised of three things. Do not engage in conversations with deluded patients; do not form relationships with them; and, peculiarly, be aware that every schizo-phrenic has a schizophrenogenic mother. It was with some relief that I happened upon Laing's account of his induction:

> The staff had strict orders not to talk to the patients or to encourage the patients to talk to them, or to each other, or to themselves, or at all. Talking between patients was observed, reported and broken up. You must not let a schizophrenic talk to you. It aggravates the psychotic process. As in bone fractures, so in fractured minds: immobilisation is the answer. (Laing 1985, p.123)

Surprisingly, the concept of schizophrenogenic mother was developed by a female psychiatrist (Reichmann):

> The schizophrenic is painfully distrustful and resentful of other people due to the severe early warp and rejection encountered in important people in his infancy and childhood, as a rule, mainly by schizophrenogenic mothers. (Reichmann 1953, p.265)

Reichmann was a compassionate psychiatrist and her beliefs in this matter reflect the extraordinary virulence which psychiatry could (and does) deploy against women. However, my point is that that the classic charge against Laing, that he had invoked 'the family' as a causal factor in the onset of schizophrenia, is only partialy true: in psychiatric practice, anti-women gremlins come with the territory and Laing simply reflected this.

Laing's relationship with his mother – who probably *was* insane – throws some light on his psychiatric outlook. He told Bob Mullan that his friend, Dr Joe Schorstein, had concluded that his mother was indeed mad when he met her. Laing was ambivalent about this: whilst he thought that she 'had been mad probably from before I was born' (Mullan 1995, p.61), he did not see her as clinically psychotic. Of course, given his particular brand of psychiatry, he could hardly say otherwise. By anybody's standards she was very unusual. She was so sexually repressed that she regarded as filth anything not immediately redolent of middle-class propriety. She considered Ronald's female liaisons outside marriage filth; licentious thoughts were filth; the visible penis – especially Laing's father's which occasionally protruded through those old style pyjamas with the buttonless flies – was filth. Even Laing's choice of medical speciality was reprehensible. Whilst Laing's father knew little about psychiatry, his mother knew that it meant confiding private thoughts to strangers, it was 'letting the world know your business', not proper doctoring at all. She neither kissed nor cuddled him in childhood and in middle age she informed him in a pencilled note that she no longer wanted him around her even in death. Laing's responses to all this are difficult to gauge. In many ways, he treated family matters in much the same way that he regarded previous work. When asked about his mother's rejection he replied, as he always did, that there was no point in plying a lost cause. Whether or not she kept a doll into which she stuck needles in the hope of inducing a heart attack in him – it worked eventually – is doubtful: when he confronted her about it she made the superb reply, 'Ronald, we don't talk about that sort of thing' (Mullan 1995, p.47).

At her funeral, he bawled his eyes out although crying during emotional moments – when reading poetry or watching movies – was something that he was wont to do: he never concealed the sensitive, vulnerable sides to his nature.

Inebriation

In later years, life bore him little charm. His influence within the medical profession (never strong) declined markedly: after all, he had embarrassed them and they had responded by throwing him off their register. By the mid-1970s, alcohol consumption had taken its toll and film footage shows an often sloshed Laing coasting on well-practised anecdotes, superficial philosophy, shameless rambling and only avoiding complete disaster by the apparent accidental production of some old 'profundity' or other. There was nothing new in this: trouble had been brewing for some time. In Chicago, in 1972, a student responded to his presentation thus:

> Doctor Laing, this is one of the largest crowds we've had here for a speaker, yet I feel we have been presented with a fumbling, rambling performance. I would like to ask: is this some sort of social experiment? Is this something by example you're showing us or is this merely something of the high stature you have for yourself and you are presenting us with any old rotten baggage and you're expecting us to applaud? (Clay 1997, pp.170–171)

On the whole, Laing's British audiences were too polite (or too frightened!) to confront him like this. In any event, Ronnie always gave as good as he got, the above questioner being told by Laing that he had 'a presumption and fucking cheek to come on in that way' and that, furthermore, had he listened 'in the right way' he would have heard the wisdom of Laing.

He could not resist conference invites: often, whilst trying to be awe-ful – a guru requirement – he was merely awful. Extraordinarily disrespectful to audiences, he cared little for their disappointment, sadness, shock or even the triumph that some felt at 'seeing through him' at last.

> 'Life, you see, is a sexually transmitted disease with a 100 per cent mortality rate'. If R.D. Laing had said that to me in the late sixties/early seventies, I would have immediately rushed away and told all my friends that the great guru had actually spoke to me and I would have pondered the meaning for ages and the deep significance in it. Tempus fugit. When he said it to me last week, I recalled having seen it on a lavatory wall some months previously and I got to thinking what exactly does it mean? I relegated it to the meaningless and ponderous statements such as 'Who digs deepest deepest digs'. I also wondered which one of us had changed. (Hilmore 1985, p.18)

It was the times that had changed. The effervescent Sixties found a welcome audience in the Seventies, an audience keen to embellish its progenitor no end. The Eighties was payback time: the restructuring of traditional lines of engagement. Had Laing not strayed beyond these lines in the first place he might have avoided the painful rejections of his later 'literary works', his weird entree into obstetrics and the mysticism which pervaded his later texts. There is an other-worldliness about his book *The Politics of Experience and the Bird of Paradise* (1967), an abandonment of mainstream thinking, which many found alarming. Not that he wasn't bothered by this. As early as 1972 he was battling to end this phase of his career. In a speech on 10 August he specifically rejected principles with which he had become famously associated. He had never said that families caused schizophrenia, he was not advocating LSD in the manner of Timothy Leary, he at no time stated that schizophrenia was a desirable state and so on. Yet even by 1972, it was too late, and to this day he is seen as having embraced all of these things.

No let up

Even in death, Laing was subjected to critical abuse; for example Anthony Daniels's (1996) jibe that his 'inebriated philosophical reach exceeded his inebriated philosophical grasp'. According to this writer, Laing had 'contributed nothing to the sum of human knowledge' and that acting on his ideas 'would only add to human misery'. This certainly indicated Ronnie's capacity to arouse strong feelings, for whatever the truth of the 'contributed nothing' remark it is an absurd assertion that his ideas always brought misery.

Many years later, when interviewed by Anthony Clare (1996) for the series *In the Psychiatrist's Chair*, Laing indeed arrived for the interview 'under the influence'. Having sobered up, however, he proceeded, as Clare observed, to give an interview full of surprisingly insightful, fresh and thoughtful comments. Bad when he needed to be, he could be good when he wanted. Single-minded to the last about one thing, before his death Laing said:

> The psychiatric, diagnostic look is itself a depersonalised and depersonalising cut-off look. It is an application of a highly sophisticated scientific look that is culturally deeply conditioned. It is a way of seeing things, and the relation between things, by subtracting all personal experience. However a person is not a thing, nor is a thing a person. It is the exact opposite of a sensibility cultivated with the express intention of recognising and sympathetically understanding the intentions of others. (in Gregory 1987, p.417)

The Sigal book

In the mid-Sixties Clancy Sigal worked with Laing in London and his experiences resulted in a novel *Zone of the Interior* (1976) which, at Laing's objection, was never published in Britain. It is not the case, as Ronnie liked to say, that no publisher would touch this 'blasphemous' book but that he made sure they couldn't (Burston 1996; Clay 1997; Laing 1994). As recently as 1990, a mooted publication invoked further mutterings of Laingian litigation. Others (Kotowicz 1997; Mullan 1995) regard Sigal's novel as scurrilous, a wicked caricature. The novel reminisces about 1960s London, a Scottish radical psychiatrist called Willie Last – will he last? – and other luminaries of the counterculture. It is impossible not to recognise the cast of characters, often hilariously so, and it is understandable that Laing wanted it kept under wraps. John Clay (1997) thought that Laing may have perceived a quasi-homosexuality between the novel's main protagonist – clearly meant to be him – and the Sigal character. Laing could be intimate with people of different genders: however this rarely extended beyond the maudlin embraces typical of inebriates. Burston (1996) notes that, whatever Sigal's animosity, the picture of Laing which emerges from his book classically fits the drug preoccupied, consciousness changing, mind expanding tenor of the times. That Laing indulged in a modest amount of pharmacological and other experimentation is not in doubt: the Kingsley Hall period, especially, permitted a fair measure of social and personal laxity. However, that Laing resembles the cynical, self-obsessed, manipulative Willie Last is less certain: it could be true.

Life

The point about any life of R.D. Laing is that you accept 'the gory bits': the off-putting mixture of crudity and sensitivity, the snatches of brilliance amidst the swagger and pretence. For as Jan Resnick recalled, 'There wasn't anyone who knew him who hadn't been offended by him at one time or another' (Resnick 1990, p.15).

For instance, he had acquired early on an aptitude to cast aside anyone who annoyed him – exceptionally so when he was under the influence – and his annoyance was provoked as much by obsequiousness as by opposition. A champagne radical, he could find himself supporting establishment 'events' whilst indulging in angry outbursts against them. For example, he attended the 1966 National Association for Mental Health Annual Meeting but then proceeded to speak in a way likely to cause offence. Yet he liked formality and ritual and enjoyed such occasions when done well. Occasionally, as in 1985 when his picture was being hung in the National Portrait Gallery of Scotland, he behaved impeccably. In general, though, rectitude was not Ronnie's forte and, ravaged by alcohol, the fall from grace became habitual.

This 'warts and all' approach is not to everyone's taste. Zbigniew Kotowicz, for one, refers to Adrian Laing's book as one where 'the reader will find ample supply of stories about Laing's complicated personal life, about his financial difficulties, about his drunken stunts but…not much else' (Kotowicz 1997, p.7). Sensitive to the thrashing which Laingian ideas had received throughout the Seventies and Eighties, Kotowicz attempted to re-establish their validity. This, of course, is important. Our interest in, let's say, Platonic ideas, is justified when they continue to be seen as relevant. In Laing's case, sustaining relevance is problematic.

Gadfly

For the most part, he was an intellectual gadfly who failed to account for important parts of his work: he wrote nothing about Kingsley Hall and said little about his practice generally other than some interviews given towards the end of his life. Commenting on his 'celebrated' failure to produce a Volume II to *Sanity, Madness and the Family, Volume 1*, he said that this was because the normal (as opposed to the mad) families of the first volume simply did not interview well. The truth is, they bored him to tears and he would later tell Bob Mullan: 'They were fucking dead and there was no edge or no sharpness or no challenge' (Mullan 1995, p.281).

In Stuart Sutherland's opinion, having failed to uncover evidence confirming his beliefs about families, he just 'dishonestly refused to publish his results' (Sutherland 1998, p.125). Danial Burston disagrees: Laing's impulse, he says, was always to move on, that he hated going over old ground. Moving on, however, meant accumulating more and more 'unfinished business' and the loss of a clear line of intellectual development or even consistency.

Aftermath: the line of attack

Thomas Szasz's (1976) savaging of Laing reminds us that anti-psychiatry was far from an homogeneous movement. This was a problem for Laing because as Szasz was spitting blood at his supposed communism, Peter Sedgwick was castigating him for having deserted the Left. Laing, however, was never specific on political issues, often protesting an inability to think in straightforward political terms. It's tempting to think that he 'ran with the hare and hunted with the hounds': the truth is, he cared little for movements other than as vehicles for perpetuating his public profile.

In everything that happened afterwards, there was as much in it for him as for his enemies. No one forced him to drink or to assert that embryos had memories. And if the combination of bad behaviour and ultimately asinine ideas failed to impress, why be surprised? Yet there was a moment around the time of *The Divided Self* when he said something about schizophrenia that was genuinely groundbreaking. However, conventionality digs its heels in when it senses more than half-hearted rebellion. The medicalists bided their time and as the giddiness of 'the Swinging Sixties' declined, scope for conformist rearmament increased.

Laing set up no school; he had few disciples. He would say that this was because his followers, such as David Cooper, were themselves unique: maybe so. In any event, the Sixties was about changing, not establishing, things, a time when social malcontents were misinterpreted as possible liberators, a shortish period in which orthodoxy seemed to be on the run but was really re-grouping itself.

So how to sum him up? Doris Lessing was right when she said that Laing changed the way we look at schizophrenia 'but no more and no less'. But this was a lot more than we (or sadly he) ever realised. If his achievement had been, as some imagine, the formulation of some Gnostic-theology of the psyche – where schizophrenia takes on elements of mystic flight – then his decline would be permanent (and deserved). Granted, Laing did indulge in the kind of intellectualising that lacks sympathy for human misery. But we can consign these failings to a weakness for adulation, the desire to impress. He couldn't bear the ordinariness of life and the drinking outmanoeuvred this, which he acknowledged: he would have recognised Dean Martin's injunction to his audiences: 'Drink up and be somebody'.

Of course, he continued to have his fans. Jacqueline Du Pre carried his book of poems *Knots* everywhere and *The Bird of Paradise* is still read by thousands. But more than that, he put the person back into psychiatric discourse: he made it respectable to believe that doubt, uncertainty, and mystery might still imbue inquiries into what it means to be psychiatrically ill. In his papers, books and at conferences he pushed the boat out in search of alternatives to (somatic) psychiatry. So what if the times were confrontational? It was a brave thing to do all the same because it entailed a forfeiture of 'place' amongst medical peers. The price tag of his achievement is that it exposed him to the wrath of those who knew all along that the truth lay elsewhere.

References

Barnes, M. and Berke, J. (1971) *Mary Barnes: Two Accounts of a Journey Through Madness.* London: MacGibbon and Kee.

Burston, D. (1996) *The Wing of Madness: The Life and Work of R.D. Laing.* Cambridge, MA: Harvard University Press.

Burston, D. (2000) *The Crucible of Experience: R.D. Laing and the Crisis of Psychotherapy.* London: Harvard University Press.

Clare, A. (1996) *In the Psychiatrist's Chair II.* London: Mandarin Books.

Claridge, G. (1990) 'Can a diseases model of schizophrenia survive?' In R.P. Bentall (ed) *Reconstructing Schizophrenia.* London: Routledge.

Clay, J. (1997) *R.D. Laing: A Divided Self.* London: Sceptre Books.

Cooper, D. (1968) *To Free a Generation: The Dialectics of Liberation.* Harmondsworth: Penguin Books.

Curtance, J. (1951) *Wisdom, Madness and Folly: Common Sense Psychiatry for Lay People.* London: Victor Gollancz.

Daniels, A. (1996) 'Where does madness lie?' *The Sunday Telegraph* 30 June, 12.

Davidson, B. (1998) 'The role of the psychiatric nurse.' In B. Davidson and P. Barker (eds) *Psychiatric Nursing: Ethical Strife.* London: Arnold.

Foucault, M. (1971) *Madness and Civilisation: A History of Insanity in the Age of Reason.* London: Tavistock Publications.

Goffman, E. (1968) *Asylums: Essays on the Social Situation of Mental Patients and other Inmates.* Harmondsworth: Penguin Books.

Gregory, R. (1987) *The Oxford Companion to the Mind.* Oxford: Oxford University Press.

Heller, J. (1962) *Catch 22.* London: Jonathan Cape.

Hilmore, P. (1985) *London Observer* 17 March, 18.

Jenner, F.A., Monteiro, A.C.D., Zagalo-Cardoso, J.A. and Cunha-Oliveira J.A. (1993) *Schizophrenia: A Disease or Some Ways of Being Human?* Sheffield: Sheffield Academic Press.

Kesey, K. (1963) *One Flew Over The Cuckoo's Nest.* London: Methuen.

Knowles, J. (2001) 'TCs – do we need to break free and think again?' *Therapeutic Communities 22,* 4, 271–285.

Kotowicz, Z. (1997) *R.D. Laing and the Paths of Anti-psychiatry.* London: Routledge.

Laing, A. (1994) *R.D. Laing: A Biography.* London: Peter Owen.

Laing, R.D. (1960) *The Divided Self: A Study in Insanity and Madness.* London: Tavistock.

Laing, R.D. (1967) *The Politics of Experience and the Bird of Paradise.* Harmondsworth: Penguin Books.

Laing, R.D. (1985) *Wisdom, Madness and Folly.* London: Macmillan.

Laing, R.D. and Esterson, A. (1970) *Sanity, Madness and the Family, Volume 1: Families of Schizophrenics.* Harmondsworth: Penguin Books.

Loach, K. (1971) *Family Life.* London: Woodfall Films.

Marwick, A. (1998) *The Sixties.* Oxford: Oxford University Press.

Mezan, P. (1972) 'After Freud and Jung, now comes R.D. Laing.' *Esquire 77,* 160–178.

Miller, J.B. (1988) *Towards a New Psychology of Women.* Harmondsworth: Penguin.

Mullan, B. (1995) *Mad to be Normal: Conversations with R.D. Laing.* London: Free Association Books.

Reed, D. (1974) *Anna.* London: Secker and Warburg.

Reichmann, F. (1953) *Principles of Intensive Psychotherapy.* London: George Allen and Unwin.

Resnick, J. (1990) 'In fact, I cannot.' *Asylum 4,* 2, 15.

Sargant, W. (1967) *The Unquiet Mind: The Autobiography of a Physician in Psychological Medicine.* London: Heinemann.

Scull, A. (1979) *Museums of Madness.* London: Allen Lane.

Sedgwick, P. (1982) *Psycho politics.* London: Pluto.

Showalter, E. (1985) *The Female Malady: Women, Madness and English Culture, 1830–1980.* London: Virago.

Sigal, C. (1976) *Zone of the Interior.* New York: Thomas Y. Crowell.

Storr, A. (1996) 'Mad about schizophrenia.' *Financial Times* 30 June, 12.

Sunday Times (1999) 'One Hundred Great Scots.' *The Sunday Times (Scotland)* 18 April – 9 May.

Sutherland, S. (1998) *Breakdown.* Oxford: Oxford University Press.

Szasz, T. (1976) *The Myth of Mental Illness.* London: Harper and Row.

Williamson, B. (1990) *The Temper of the Times: British Society Since World War II.* London: Basil Blackwell.

Yellowlees, H. (1953) *To Define True Madness.* London: Sidgwick and Jackson.

Young, R. (1966) 'The divided science.' *Delta 38,* 13–18.

CHAPTER 7

The Importance of Being Anti

Mental hospitals flourish on uncertainty – what treatment one is going to receive, what ward one is going to be transferred to, whether or not one is going to be discharged – or if one is ever going to be discharged.

David Cooper (1967)

Beginnings

When Villa 21 began as an experimental therapeutic community at Shenley Hospital, London, in 1962 – experimental in that it comprised mainly schizophrenic patients – there were about 130 psychiatric hospitals in England and Wales of which more than 100 contained in excess of 1000 patients each. I mention this so as to indicate the broader context against which such experiments took place. The herding together of large numbers of people had led – necessarily perhaps – to the imposition of fixed procedures for doing things: procedures which, remarkably quickly, became heavily institutionalised, with a neglect of basic civilities and even, on occasions, verbal and physical abuse of patients. Although unremittingly harsh, in many respects this is not the complete picture and some of these hospitals developed into benevolent dynasties, a state of affairs captured best by David Clark:

> Everyone knew how mental hospitals should be – custodial but humane –
> an enclosed world where nothing changed from generation to generation,
> where long-stay patients and staff grew old together watching cricket,
> enjoying social events such as balls and dances and regarding innovations
> with distaste. (in Barham 1997, p.158)

For David Cooper, however, these hospitals had few redeeming features, especially the ones surrounding London which were particularly dire. Cooper went to Shenley in 1960 with a set of beliefs that comprehensively denied every precept of conventional psychiatry. In particular, he jeered at the notion of psychiatry as an objective medical speciality which dealt with factual entities called mental illnesses. For Cooper, *everything* had a political dimension and the struggle – and, for him, it *was* a struggle – was to combat the malevolence which psychiatrists foisted on their hospitalised victims.

Changes

By 1962, considerable innovation had already taken place within British mental hospitals. However, the tendency to view these changes as a generalised or systematic progression is mistaken. Change varied from hospital to hospital as well as from ward to ward, with progress in unlocking wards, for example, coming at a price: relative liberty for patients here but with increasing seclusion for likely troublemakers there. Such trade-offs were common but if they resulted in a more civilised regime overall, then why not? Villa 21 was certainly not a product of general psychiatric progressivism; instead, its beginnings sprang from a radicalism which had germinated outside the NHS. The principal account of the unit's commissioning and 'progress' is by Cooper (1967), its founder and medical director, being part of his general text *Psychiatry and Anti-psychiatry*. Although informative, its literary style combines 'sociologese' and existentialism in equal measure and whilst this has an occasional abrasive elegance, accommodating to it takes time. The style is lampooned by Clancy Sigal in his novel *Zone of the Interior* (1976) of which more later. Sigal worked at the Villa and he satirises not just Cooper's dialogue but also the motives of those involved and their sincerity.

Comparing Cooper's account with accounts of other communities (see Campling and Haigh 1999) one is struck by the survivalist, embattled tone of having to withstand external pressures as well as an apprehension of sabotage from within. For Villa 21, there was an added dimension, *in extremis*, of confronting one's own resistance to change and the psychoanalytic implications thereof. Part of the unit's function, therefore, was to formalise strategies so as to counter staff resistance and render it inactive.

Shenley: the parent hospital

In 1962, the patient population of Shenley Hospital was 2100 and Cooper was now two years into his post. Unusually, for an NHS psychiatrist, he espoused a blend of Marxism and existentialism (perhaps in that order). He saw schizophrenia as a 'violence' visited upon people by a capitalist system which depended for its survival on removing anyone not self-sufficient. The schizophrenic was akin to the revolutionary since he refused the legitimacy of conventional mores; moral, political or social. He – and it was always a he – was the ultimate 'outsider', the 'outsider' metaphor (Wilson 1956) preoccupying intellectuals (and the popular media) at the time. R.D. Laing, we may recall, was angry that Colin Wilson had got the jump on him by publishing *The Outsider* which, at first, was thought by many to be a work of genius. Wilson's book purported to show some characters from history and fiction – T.E. Lawrence, Blake, Sartre – who were not fully invested in society but whose case *against* society is very clear:

> All men and women have these dangerous, unnameable impulses, yet they keep up a pretence, to themselves, to others; their respectability, their philosophy, their religion, are all attempts to gloss over, to make look civilised and rational something that is savage, unorganised, irrational. He is an Outsider because he stands for Truth. (Wilson 1956, p.13)

In some ways, Wilson's book was merely a confused resume of philosophy in the Niezscian/Existential tradition to which he had added the rhetorical flourish of 'Outsider'. Masters saw it as:

> a long philosophical essay in the manner of Albert Camus, dealing with people who were observers of life rather than participators, not, as the psychiatrists would maintain because they were neurotic, but because they saw and understood too much of life's essential absurdity without being able to do anything about it. (Masters 1985, p.133)

Although later criticised, the book was initially influential and its bearing on anti-psychiatric thinking has perhaps been overlooked. Although existentialism was strewn across the pages of continental (philosophy) journals its introduction to British audiences by a group of anti-psychiatrists was remarkable. They argued that existentialism bore directly on discussions about schizophrenia and they started by depicting schizophrenics as Kafaesque captives of a threatened society: unable to match desires to surroundings, the schizophrenic 'concludes' that a retreat (from society, from self) is the best option. Cooper construed Villa 21 as a place where withdrawal could take place with minimal interference from society or its psychiatric agents. Extraordinarily, he lacked all sense of irony that he too was a psychiatrist setting up a treatment milieu, however fluid its boundaries might be. Perhaps this explains his eagerness to denote himself and others (much to their annoyance) as 'anti-psychiatrists' as if to derail them, ethically and professionally, from everyday theory and practice.

At this point, it might help to look at what was meant by 'anti-psychiatrist'. Cooper provided little in the way of definition and the reader is referred to chapter five of *The Grammar of Living* where there is a lengthy description. The gist of it goes like this:

Perhaps the most central characteristic of anti-psychiatry is the recognition of the need for attentive non-interference aimed at *the opening up of experience rather than its closing down* [his italics]. The condition for the possibility of this is being with the right other people, that is to say with people who have sufficiently explored their own interiority and their own despair. (Cooper 1976, p.56)

Throughout psychiatric history, the pre-eminence of 'the subjective' has been a fundamental principle for psychiatric dissidence, the argument being that psychiatrists have no logical or moral grounds to treat people as if their experiences didn't count, that psychotic illnesses are simply other ways of being human. That conventional psychiatrists intentionally dehumanised people in the way Cooper said they did is by no means clear: unwittingly, perhaps, they did but that is not the same thing. Further, having defined the schizophrenic as an outsider/revolutionary it was never made clear how this person differs from, say, political activists (of either the Left or Right) and there were certainly enough of those at the time whom psychiatry left well enough alone. Why those diagnosed as schizophrenic were 'chosen' from the broad sweep of 'revolutionaries' who were not, was rarely discussed.

The Villa

Shenley Hospital was typical: large, foreboding and socially introverted, a temple of alienation, estrangement and subtle violence. It was an inauspicious place for an experiment; an ageing Villa, formerly an insulin coma ward – comas induced by insulin injections being a schizophrenia treatment at the time. However, capital expenditure for new buildings was unavailable and, besides, other hospitals, equally archaic, equally inauspicious, had fostered enterprising shifts in patterns of care. True, Villa 21 bore the hallmarks of a peculiar radicalism. To begin with, the patients were mainly schizophrenics, the group classically regarded as epitomising madness. For Cooper, however, schizophrenia was:

a micro-social crisis situation in which the acts and experience of a certain person are invalidated by others for certain intelligible cultural and micro-cultural reasons, to the point where he is elected and identified as being mentally ill in a certain way, and is then confirmed in the identity of schizophrenic patient by medical or quasi-medical agents. (Cooper 1967, p.2)

Why anyone would 'invite' such a categorisation, either from his family or from psychiatrists, is left unsaid: 'I assume no primary defect in the patient-to-be but would suggest that there is a demonstrable failure in a micro-social field of persons in relation' (Cooper 1967, p.2). At the time this was written, 'self' psychology was habitually characterised as 'selves in relation', the psychological lives of individuals increasingly seen as caught up in social and specifically family processes. Cooper was by far the most unambiguous exponent of this view and whilst his circuitous syntax belies it, his was the most consistently clear exposition of non-medical psychiatry.

The clientele

You might consider that when Villa 21 hit difficulties it was because of its clientele. The merger of schizophrenia and therapeutic community practice was, after all, both daring and dangerous. Broadly speaking, Cooper saw it as freeing patients from administrative rigidity so that they could have better contact with each other, come to know themselves better, and not spiral down into the burnt-out states that were part and parcel of the hospitals.

The staff knew that there would be problems: there was a risk of the Villa becoming a receptacle into which hostile outsiders would project all kinds of 'badness', that it could become a scapegoat for problems that were actually hospital wide. Schoenberg (1980) had described this phenomenon in the wider context where hospitals exist as 'castles of fantasy' into which outside groups project their loathing and fear. In time, the unit came to serve this function for an increasingly perplexed and angry hospital albeit they would no doubt say that this was less projection and more a fact of the unit coming apart.

The patients were late adolescent and early adult males, most having been independently diagnosed as schizophrenic. Schizophrenia is an elastic diagnosis but is nevertheless asserted, by psychiatrists, to consist of delusions and hallucinations which make rational thought by affected individuals extremely difficult. Accordingly, unless the individual takes anti-psychotic medication (usually for life and with many undesirable effects) the illness proceeds towards chronicity and profound disability. The anti-psychiatrists took a diametrically opposing view, declaring schizophrenia an understandable reaction to hostile social events and mediated principally through families, the hallucinations and delusions being explicable as strategies designed to make sense of the hostility.

Beginnings

The intention was to select nurses who would be less 'institutionally deformed' and so better able to participate in group therapy with minimal anxiety. One charge and one staff nurse were picked for each of the two shifts and student nurses would also work on the unit as part of their training. It was believed important that the experiment be seen as not too 'far out' and, to that end, a vigilant eye was kept on the wider hospital community. In this instance, the selection of Frank Atkin as charge-nurse was crucial since he was trusted not only by David Cooper but by the Shenley Hospital authorities as well. Ironically, Cooper writes that, 'The original programme of the unit was deliberately a highly structured one, not unlike that of the classical therapeutic community' (Cooper 1967, p.86).

Whilst not unsympathetic to therapeutic community ideals, Cooper wanted to journey further and probably, ultimately, dismantle the therapeutic enterprise altogether. He was alert to the seductions of liberal psychiatry, its capacity to claim ownership of new ideas and, in the process, rob them of their cutting edge.

> Most apparent psychiatric progress expressed in the catchwords open doors, permissiveness, informality, friendly staff-patient relations, serves to obscure this far more central idea in which the traditional psychiatric hospital has not advanced one inch since the days of Kraepelin in the last century. (Cooper 1967, p.28)

This we might now see more clearly with hindsight: that whilst there existed pockets of progress, what we would now call 'centres of excellence', the overall conditions of hospitals were still awful and made more difficult to attack by the celebrity status of some smaller units.

Group therapy and the nursing imperative

As we saw in Chapter 5, precise definitions of therapeutic communities are difficult although most would agree that a certain blurring of roles between staff and patients is a pre-requisite. Therefore, if there are some who do not share this belief or are made uncomfortable by it, then conflict will result. For example, in contemporary forensic units, some of which call themselves therapeutic communities, determining 'correct' relationships between nurses and patients is riddled with conflict. This conflict is exacerbated if therapeutically oriented nurses seek to convene staff groups with the purpose of 'exploring their own feelings'. I reported (Clarke 1996) on one such unit where some nurses had refused participation in groupwork stating that they were 'not patients', a viewpoint asserted with vernacular vigour. In effect, they saw self-reflection as a symbolic fracturing of the glass that separated them from the patients.

Cooper had made it clear that in setting up Villa 21 his central conviction 'was that before we have any chance of understanding what goes on in patients we have to have at least some elementary awareness about what goes on in the staff' (Cooper 1967, p.87–88).

Later, he states that, 'The real difficulty for staff is to confront themselves, to confront their own problems, disturbances, madness. Each one has to risk meeting the lunatic in himself' (Cooper 1967, p.103) The way to run that risk is by coming together to unravel, expose and dispel it. Noticeably, Cooper excludes himself from this and, reading his descriptions of staff morbidity, one longs for the word 'we' to materialise but it doesn't. Other things are avoided too: the possibility that some patients might be hearing voices instructing them to do harm is denied: the mechanisms by which both groups – staff and patients – have ended up in hospital, in terms of real differences between them, and in terms of how they are perceived socially, is also not examined. Such differences exist and yet no distinction is made between the medical 'illusions' of staff and schizophrenic patients who, in his view, they have dominated, categorised and generally invalidated. The point is, what is it that gives one group ascendancy over the other? How has one group been rendered vulnerable to psychiatric invalidation across almost two centuries? That powerful socio-political forces may be at play is not the question: rather it is about working out why some people are susceptible to these forces in a particular way and others not.

Convictions

In his book, *Psychiatry and Anti-psychiatry,* Cooper states:

> The psychiatric institution throughout its history has found it necessary to defend itself against the madness which it is supposed to contain – disturbance, disintegration, violence, contamination. The staff defences, in so far as they are erected against illusory rather than real dangers, I shall term collectively *institutional irrationality.* What then, is the reality of madness in the mental hospital and what is illusion? (Cooper 1967, p.88)

His answer is seriously deficient: having posed the question, he immediately launches into an anecdote about burly policemen carrying straightjacketed patients from one room to the next. Then, admitting that straightjackets are a thing of the past, he suggests that electric treatment and drugs are their natural heirs and successors. There are similarities. For example, he makes a fair point that patients are often un-informed about why they are being medicated and he also correctly identifies the coercion that is ritually visited on any patient who wishes to stay in bed longer than staff will allow. I will return to the latter point shortly. In designating drugs as 'chemical straightjackets', however, there is actually an important distinction to be made. The straightjacket did, like drugs, control patients' behaviour, true. However, its sole intent was to quell violence or imminent violence. Whereas drugs are sometimes used with this in mind, they also have longer-term effects. For instance, they can diminish depression, alleviate voices, curtail delusions and moderate anxiety. Psychiatric service users such as Ron Coleman (1999) have attested this un-ambiguously without compromising their general scepticism about psychiatry.

On the question of patients refusing to leave their beds, it is noticeable how this arouses anxiety in nurses, being conceived, perhaps, as a rejection of nursing legitimacy. At Villa 21 there was vigorous opposition to patients 'having a lie-in' but a 'hands off' approach eventually prevailed because, as Cooper and Atkin anticipated, the patients eventually got themselves up even if, in some cases, the process took weeks! Adopting this stance was risky and required self-conviction and tenacity. Whilst Cooper did not lack the former, he began to run short of the latter when the hospital withdrew support. Why this happened is difficult to assess since Cooper's account is poor on detail whilst heavy on (psycho) analysis. Luckily, we have Clancy Sigal's novel *Zone of the Interior* (1976) which is partly based on Sigal having worked at the Villa.

An insider's view

The novel confirms much that we already know about Villa 21. For example, that it did abolish the menial tasks which had constituted the typical Shenley Hospital patients' day. Far from preventing institutionalisation, getting patients to do monotonous Industrial Unit work was believed to foster deterioration and chronicity. Few people who experienced these units will doubt their capacity to induce instant tedium. The work was pernickety and repetitive comprising things like straightening out bent metal filaments or packing items into empty boxes. The Villa 21 solution was disarmingly downbeat: all industrial 'therapy' was stopped. However, some of the reasoning that lay behind this had about it an offhand tone:

> there is something remarkably healthy about the chronic schizophrenic, preoccupied with his inner world, spending the day hunched over the central heating fitting in a decrepit back ward. If he does not have the solution to the riddle of life, at least he has fewer illusions. (Cooper 1967, p.90)

The struggles of psychotic people are being philosophically skirted around here with a disregard about how it might feel to be 'hunched over' a radiator, in poor living conditions for long periods of time. Cooper's remarks contain insincerity and an inability, perhaps unwillingness, to look at things comprehensively. His remarks are hardly rhetorical and we have lots of evidence of patients in his care being left to their own devices. For example, in Sigal's novel a fight breaks out between two patients but the nurses continue to play cards until the storm blows itself out. The strategy works – the fight evaporates – and the message is that the less staff 'interfere', the more will social process take its course. At one point, Les O'Brian, a charge nurse with 20 years' experience in mental hospitals, says that 'mental nursing is knowing when *not* to act at times of crises or mass anxiety' (Sigal 1976, p.58).[1] It's a high risk endeavour but this time it has a solid history within good therapeutic community practice.

Trouble

All mental health provision is an expression of its national culture. Interviewed in 1983, it was Cooper's view that:

> In many third world countries and in the south of Italy and parts of Europe, there is a relatively intact community matrix. People still know how to talk to each other. The communicational matrix has been largely destroyed in Northern Europe in the so-called post industrial world. (Lacey 1983, p.9)

The idea is that the walk-in centres which opened in parts of Italy, following hospital closures, were successful because Italians are more easygoing than are British people whose predilections infect relationships with a certain reserve as well as complex rules for the governance of this reserve. Rules become important especially when people come together by circumstance or accident as is often the case with therapeutic communities. Without rules, imaginations run riot and mechanisms are needed to deal with the anxiety that comes from this. For example, Isabel Menzies (1960) observed how hospital nurses generated routinised tasks so as to ward off anxiety that accrued from too close contact with patients. This is a productive way to discuss anxiety but it presupposes acceptance of psychoanalytic principles and this is difficult where there exists, in the culture, an inherent tendency to privacy and keeping a stiff upper lip. It is not that psychoanalysis doesn't explain this as much as that its explanatory power is resisted and even denigrated. This resistance extends to psychiatric staff who, perceiving a loss of control over their work – and therapeutic community work implies such a loss – may become unduly anxious and seek to re-establish control surreptitiously. This, however, seems not to have happened at Villa 21 where the nurses, led by Frank Atkin, made challenging psychological principles work, at least for a while.

When Villa 21 started to fall apart, it was not through any objections to its theoretical principles – that would come later – as much as that the place began to smell. Some of the patients had 'chosen' not to engage in mundane tasks like washing up and the collapse in hygiene was becoming too much for some. Shanley (1999) recalls that some nurse managers were refusing to enter the Villa because of this and that communication sometimes took place through an open window. Patients were free to do much as they pleased albeit they had to remain within the unit unless given permission to leave. Masturbating publicly was not allowed nor was walking around naked: other than that, most behaviour was acceptable. There was some faeces smeared here and there but, in true therapeutic community style, it wasn't considered to be the staff's responsibility to clear it up. The ideology was that patients create (and so live within) their own reality: cleaning up after them would violate their space.

Unsurprisingly, pressure from the hospital mounted. In Pullen's opinion (1999) this was understandable as the consequences of not washing up for weeks began to manifest itself and meant that food could no longer be cooked. Cooper later told an interviewer: 'All the conventional methods of control were being discarded. Nurses had to adopt a different attitude' (Lacey 1983, p.8). The reality, however, was that nurses were being asked to abandon not just custodialism but many of life's basic civilities and this in a context where nursing was traditionally the guardian of hospital morality and etiquette.

> What was going on in the Villa was of course provocative, revaluing by implication the life's work of other staff and challenging all the defences they relied on to survive. In such circumstances envy, hostility and, yes, persecution will be aroused. It is not easy to deal with these forces: Cooper quit. (Pullen 1999, p.148)

A degree of antagonism had existed between the two nursing shifts with one more accepting of the experiment than the other. Because of the tendency (at the time) to invest medics with omnipotence those opposing the experiment saw it as 'the doctor's policy'. The task of decentralising power, of instigating some kind of collective ownership, was not working. The rules of the parent hospital in respect of hygiene, attendance at meetings (patients had previously decided not to attend) and the granting of week-end leave were re-implemented with Cooper's reluctant agreement. Responding to the pressures from senior nurses outside the unit, he said, 'The demand to re-establish controls and tidy up things assumed the dimensions of a desperate struggle between life and death forces, sanity and madness' (Cooper 1967, p.98).

Questions from within

To challenge psychiatric authority from inside hospital systems was to court psychological disaster: indeed, resistance to hospital authority was often seen as evidence of instability. I recall one of my psychiatric tutors replying to an inquiry about anti-psychiatrists by saying that they 'were all mad' and, at Villa 21, this view prevailed about some of those supporting the experiment. Given that the hospital administrators who sought the unit's closure also controlled appointments and promotions, the nurses who supported the experiment were brave. Almost nothing is known about them, apart from Frank Atkin, one of the charge nurses who has not been given the credit he deserves:

> Those who knew Villa 21, including Aaron Esterson, Mary Garvey, Sid Briskin and Clancy Sigal, all testify to Frank Atkin being a very special individual who had a way with extremely disturbed individuals. Their collective view is that Villa 21 would probably not have got off the ground without Frank's involvement. (Laing 1997, p.87)

Cooper refers to him a couple of times (never by name) but Atkin himself – typical of nurses then – published nothing. Mary O'Callaghan (formerly Garvey), who worked at Villa 21, recalls:

> When I think of the Villa, it is Frank I see. David's place was important and his was the ultimate authority but it was Frank, with his easy authority and anarchic style, the vitality of his engagement with the idea, his refusal to take refuge in false distinctions or to pretend to an absence of real ones, it was he who was at the centre of that little community, the presiding genius of Villa 21. (O'Callaghan Hernton 2003)

Apart from this, the only account of Atkin is through the fictional Les O'Brian who struts the pages of Sigal's novel *Zone of the Interior*.

The big con

In this novel, Villa 21 is called Conolly House, or Con House for short, and thereby hangs a tale. Here, the Villa is described as ramshackle and lacking direction. Cooper – called in the novel Dr Dick Drummond – is said to be 'as fond of dialectical contradictions as of rich food' (p.30). Never using one word where 20 will do, he addresses anything that comes his way in Marxist-cum-Sartrean terms. For Drummond – and as Cooper himself once said – there are no personal problems, only political ones. Yet, from early in the novel, excessive alcohol consumption is underway and some of those involved are bedevilled by domestic and personal traumas. This corroborates Adrian Laing's (1994) observation that by the time Kingsley Hall was being set up, three years after Villa 21, Cooper (and others) were having nervous and/or marriage breakdowns.

Within Conolly House (Villa 21) Drummond's contribution is that of an interested dabbler, drifting in and out at will, pontificating on the activities of some of the residents and staff rather than genuinely engaging with them. When problems begin and external criticisms mount he seems unable to take a concerted hold on what is happening. The nursing and medical staff cease to be a united front: from the novelty of the experiment there develops dissolution and feelings of threat. When Les O'Brian tries to explain what's happening he traces some of the dilemmas which therapeutic communities face within hostile environments:

> We may see ourselves as an oasis of sanity in a desert of medical ignorance. But we're still connected to [the hospital] by a thousand ties of salary, promotion, law. Just plain proximity. We can't belch without instant repercussions elsewhere. Ripples of anxiety starting in Con House – a broken window, a dirty floor or fistfight – are like a tidal wave when they hit the doors of the Chief Nurse and Divisional Heads. (Sigal 1976, p.125)[1]

Clancy Sigal had gone to Villa 21 – having been in therapy with Laing – in the hope of gaining experience of institutional psychiatry. In the novel he goes by the name of Sidney Bell. He is greeted, and treated, with suspicion by the nursing staff. Says Les O'Brian, 'Good evening *Mister* Bell, Dr Dick's not around tonight. Will any of us plebs do?' (Sigal 1976, p.34). The self-deprecation is palpable as is the ambivalence about what is going on and, particularly, relationships with Dick Drummond. Continuing to welcome Sid Bell, O'Brian obliquely defines the nurses' role as he does so: 'Ah ha, a new recruit to the cause. I know what Dick tells you innocents about this joint. But we're the slobs who have to pick up the pieces after you go' (Sigal 1976, p.34).[1]

Any nurse who reads Sigal will instantly recognise the 'off the wall' banter which characterises psychiatric nurses, a group not known for speaking its mind up front. As we saw in Chapter 2, nurses tend to hoard their thinking on different issues, only coming alive when in their own company.

O'Brian, however, needs no coaxing and talks freely about the unit and its problems:

> This unit exists on a knife edge. Everybody from ward orderly to Regional Board chairman has heard, or think they've heard, about us here. For every yank pseudoshrink who drops out of the sky to temporarily feel us up, there are ten hospital brass hats itching to bury us. We make them nervous. At least half my job is to keep them from getting *too* nervous. (Sigal 1976, p.58)[1]

By all accounts he succeeded.

Shanley (1999) confirms the stories of Frank Atkin's (Les O'Brian's) activities in swapping roles with patients, for example climbing into their beds or allowing them to wear his white coat. Sigal, although not a nurse, has an affinity for O'Brian and the problems he and the other nurses face: he seems to understand the awkward position they are in, particularly when having to cope with other disciplines, a position well known in the nursing literature (see Towell 1975).

> We're like the man on th' flying trapeze. Frantically swinging between Dick's revolution and the orthodoxy of the other doctors. And nobody's down below waiting to catch us either just patients dying to see us lose our grip. Eventually we become as mystified as the most deluded back ward zombie. (Sigal 1976, p.58)[1]

On the question of treatments in Con House, Sid Bell is surprised to discover that psychiatric drugs are not excluded and it again falls to O'Brian to disabuse him of the idealised expectations stemming from his association with Drummond and the other anti-psychiatrists: 'Sure we dope 'em up if we have to. What'd you expect – the millennium?' (Sigal 1976, p.35).[1]

There are, nevertheless, indications that the nurses at Villa 21 did share in the radicalism: at one point Les O'Brian tries to explain to Bell his definition of madness:

> The true definition of madness, dear sir, is that you get caught. Found out, arrested, admitted, diagnosed. The clever ones around here play possum, kiss a little arse and get out. Jerry isn't so clever. He's honest. Just a nice

English working class lad who's made one mistake too many. And keeps making the same small mistake on and on and on. (Sigal 1976, p.35)[1]

Patently, the schizophrenic is somehow 'in on the act' although we are not told whose act it is. Part of the nurses' problem was that, at Drummond's instigation, they ceded responsibility for managing patients' activities and, in effect, they left themselves with little to do:

> This place undermines us now, says O'Brian, our idea of ourselves, our job... Nobody around here wants to do themselves out of a job. So the whole sordid nonsense of patient confirming doctor in the doctor's disconfirmation of the patient endeavouring to keep staff sane who must keep patients mad – everybody's conning everybody else – never ends. (Sigal 1976, p.59)[1]

Perhaps this is the nature of the *con*: I had thought that we were meant to see Drummond as some a kind of con man. O'Brian puts a different spin on things: here, the con becomes inevitable, everyone getting caught up in the game of playing assigned roles in order simply to survive. What remains problematic is that it was to be the unit's task to see through this and do something about it. O'Brian sees the problem and, in his fashion, tries to do something about it. In the novel, he is the unit's main articulator of the irony inherent in the contradictory set-up whereby a declared anti-psychiatry tries to deal with psychosis by means of applied psychiatry. The impression of Drummond (Cooper), alternatively, is of someone writing out an apparently complex prescription of existentialism and Marxism but for an array of problems requiring more down-to-earth solutions. Thus was Atkin able to step into the breach, taking on board some of Cooper's ideas but putting a pragmatic spin on them and making them applicable and even plausible. O'Callaghan (formerly Garvey) says that when she arrived at the unit, in 1963, Frank Atkin was a figure of real authority. Cooper had had him promoted to charge-nurse, being aware of his independence of mind and capacity to implement the kinds of ideas that the other nurses would have shied away from. It was Atkin who:

> Pushed David's ideas to their logical conclusion. It was a partnership in which David got more than he had bargained for. Which is not to say that he was unhappy about it, just not quite sure what had hit him. (O'Callaghan 2003)

The family

If anything united British anti-psychiatrists it was distaste for families. Whilst Laing, as per usual, blew hot and cold on the issue, Cooper had no hesitations; he loathed 'the family' and wrote venomous after venomous tract identifying the nuclear family as the root of all evils. Families represent an unremitting attack on the 'self': they are the means by which human individuality is crushed. The child becomes unable to live by its own precepts but develops dependencies on significant others and thus is robbed of any chance of independent development. For Cooper, families were instruments of violence – ideological conditioning devices – which blamed, scapegoated and smothered their elected victims. He describes how this is done:

> There seem to be few *mothers* [my italics] who can keep their hands off their child long enough to allow the capacity to be alone to develop. There is always a need to try to arrest the wailing desperation of the other – for one's own sake if not for theirs. (Cooper 1971, p.15)

The suggestion is that when the mother goes to the distressed child this will incur 'A violation of the temporalisation...of the other so that the mother's needs gets imposed on the infant's' (Cooper 1971, pp.15–16). However, unlike, say, behaviourism, which posits a surprisingly similar framework, Cooper's theorising simply stops in mid-air: for the behaviourist, advising parents to ignore a wailing child is aimed at lessening the intensity and/or frequency of the wailing which is presumed to be psychological in origin, but, with Cooper, the task is to liberate ourselves from both the family that is 'out there' – the actual family unit – and the family 'in our heads', and we achieve this by phenomenologically *seeing through it*, by seeing it for the capitalist put up job it is. To what end we do this or what we replace the family with is left to the Gods.

Cooper could have called on some mainstream thinking in support of his views: the 1967 BBC Reith Lectures, given by Sir Edmund Leach, contended that families *had* become too inward looking: modern housing had distorted family life, cutting it off from outside influences.

> Today...there is an intensification of emotional stress between husband and wife, parents and children. The strain is greater than most of us can bear. Far from being the basis of the good society, the family with all its tawdry secrets and narrow privacy is the source of all our discontents. (in Wilson 1985, pp.30–31)

Leach's assertion that families 'incubated hate' created a furore amongst many of those concerned with rising divorce rates, the evident alienation of the young, and the lack of anything worthwhile, as they saw it, with which to substitute family life. One could, as Mary Farmer (1979) argues, equally see rising divorce rates and controlled numbers of offspring as a positive means of rescuing families, taking some of the heat out of them and giving them less to worry about.

From today's standpoint, it seems remarkable that Cooper got away with so facile a description of family life. To begin with, his attacks were typically visited upon 'the family', an abstract entity that is seldom described in any detail, and when it is, with much confusion. Skolnick (1973, p.436), for example, notes that Cooper dedicated his most virulent anti-family book to his family which had, he said, treated him with kindness during a low period 'just as a true family should'. In addition, he was also a husband and a father so that we may well ask how serious he was about what he wrote, or was he simply prone to bouts of intellectual bravura?

D.H.J. Morgan (1975) notes the 'take it or leave it' tone of much of this anti-family writing and that such sloganeering was hardly likely to engender debate. Cooper's musings rarely extended beyond speculation: it made perfect armchair psychiatry. He also avoided sources which might have enriched the debate: for instance, there was little attribution of socio-economic or cultural dimensions to the families under discussion. Presumably we are meant to generalise from the nuclear family of western capitalism to the rest of the world. Institutions were being attacked but indiscriminately, without any 'Particularised social and historical location through which universal processes have to be channelled if they are to be truly explanatory' (Martin 1970, p.191).

On the specific question of schizophrenia and its family causation, the mechanisms by which the individual *becomes* schizophrenic are unexamined: we are told *ad nauseum* of the oppressive family forces which induce madness in families and, yes, there is a sense in which families in and of themselves are repressive. But *which* factors pertaining to *which* individuals (within families) operate to produce the 'elected victim' is left unclear. Conversely, the factors which disarm or deflect families in respect of those members who 'escape' the blaming process and thus remain 'well' are also unexplained.

Of the various attempts to deal with the 'problem' of the family, none is more celebrated than the hippie commune with its multiple and shared parenting and, supposedly, sharing of everything else. These communes were few and far between in Britain, however. In many ways, they were lay people's therapeutic communities with their egalitarianism and communalism. Whilst they symbolised the attack on the nuclear family, what they meant for children, in practice, was that instead of being shouted at by one parent, you were now shouted at by the many.

Soul man

To Adrian Laing (1997), Cooper was a revolutionary romantic; he was also his father's 'soul brother', even if he invariably competed with his father for the intellectual limelight. They did get on well and, for a while, Cooper was Laing's sidekick, his 'existentialist bible, able to quote page and verse from Sartre which he seemed to know word for word' (Clay 1996, pp.85–86). Ronnie Laing liked Cooper but didn't like his books, which he found a bit embarrassing. Nor did he admire Cooper's penchant for labelling things. It was in his introduction to the 1968 anthology *The Dialectics of Liberation Conference* that Cooper branded Laing (and others) anti-psychiatrists, much to Laing's chagrin. He knew, of course, that Laing wouldn't *really* be furious, that he would enjoy the notoriety whilst protesting the label. However, Cooper *could* be difficult to get along with: he did not always see eye to eye with his fellow radicals – they were not radical *enough*. Even Laing found him difficult and a bit far-fetched. Says Adrian Laing: 'He was anti-everything: anti-apartheid, anti-hospitals, anti-universities, anti-schools, anti-prisons, anti-society, anti-families, anti-psychiatry' (Laing 1997, p.86), and its not hard to imagine that, given time, he would have come out as anti-anti. But although contemptuous of most things, he reserved an agonised repugnance for conventional norms of psychiatry and madness. Villa 21 was his opportunity to show the world: the Sixties was his time and he was going to create something groundbreaking. His vision was to delineate the role of schizophrenic as victim, one who sacrifices 'personal autonomous existence' so that families can live without guilt. To achieve this, he wanted to abolish traditional psychiatric roles and, to that end, he demanded that staff examine the 'preconceptions, prejudices, and fantasies' that they have about each other as well as their patients.

We can see, now, the political naivety with which he went about this. His assessment of the pros and cons of institutional psychiatry was fine, and not that dissimilar from conventional therapeutic community practitioners such as Maxwell Jones and David Clark. What differed was that these others, perhaps through their war experiences, had kept faith in people's goodwill. Cooper had little belief in people's capacity for altruism or compassion; as a result, he constantly thought in declarative, quixotic, terms. He had many of the qualities of the ideologue: we saw some of these in Bierer (Chapter 3), in some of Laing and in almost all of Szasz. Martin puts it well:

You cannot talk with a man who throws his sincerity at you and who persistently implies that you and every other person who disagrees with him is a racialist, an anti-Semite and a crass authoritarian. (Martin 1970, p.205)

Yet, this doesn't do justice to the *effects* of Villa 21. Whilst anti-psychiatric rhetoric has not stood the test of time, it did undermine conventional psychiatry. Anti-psychiatric tracts were not written in a vacuum but reflected a desire to change the often dehumanised conditions of mentally ill people. Further, had Cooper *not* gone on the attack, had he not been provocative, he would have been dismissed with even greater ease than he eventually was.

The myth of failure

Cooper's anti-cs eventually led him up blind alleys. In a conventionally written text *The Grammar of Living* he expressed a 'total opposition to the conventional form of writing books'. Such an activity, he opined:

can lead only to the enslavement of the minds of both the so-called writer and the so-called reader. It is a method of social control, a method of micro-political manipulation of persons, which in an exploitative society, can only lead to a false mutuality – a mutuality of exploitation that reinforces the system that oppresses us all. (Cooper 1976, pp.7–8)

He seems not to have noticed that books have been mankind's best safeguard against oppression: instead, he has arrived at the absurdist position where books have become 'exploitative acts'.

Summing up

As anti-psychiatric fervour waned, and as the 1980s loomed, he went to live in France. He found French society more receptive to his ideas particularly since, at the time, there was growing fascination with French intellectuals with their distrust of grand theories. Foucault (1971), especially, was winning a following with his sweeping claims about psychiatry's discrimination against, and marginalisation of, 'the mad'.

In any event, Cooper had long since thrown caution to the winds and must have realised that the Sixties anti-road show was over. He may have anticipated that his admission (Cooper 1967, p.94) to sleeping with a schizophrenic patient might get him into trouble. That it didn't can only mean that people had stopped listening or caring. Although the admission is couched in

the usual form of 'reaching out to a troubled spirit' it still constitutes an un-warranted violation of a vulnerable person.

Concerning Villa 21, Geoff Pullen (1999) refers to the 'myth' of its failure which originated, he says, with Kennard's account of therapeutic communities published in 1983. Pullen notes that Kennard's book was published at a time of pessimism and that today we are more upbeat about the role of communities within general psychiatric care. How ironic that Cooper, alone amongst the anti-psychiatrists, published the kinds of outcome figures that would win favour today. To some extent, his brand of psychiatry, always conscious of the political dynamics of 'care', survives: we see its capacity to agitate and disarm in movements such the 'Hearing Voices Network' and, even more so, in groups such as 'Mad Pride'. Psychiatry is always in need of a 'thorn in the side' and Cooper was certainly that. But in desiring to supplant psychiatry altogether he came unstuck; beyond the rhetoric of abolition there was little description of what a psychiatry free society might look like. To have provided that would have required explaining *why* some people behave in a psychotic manner; why, if they did not need psychiatry, as he repeatedly insisted they didn't, did they need *his* psychiatry?

Earlier, he had written:

> The 'alcoholic' of course does not exist any more than 'the junkie' or 'the schizophrenic'. My use of these essentialistic words is nothing more than an ironic reflection on the misuse of language against people. (Cooper 1976, p.137)

He died in Paris in July 1986, virtually drowning in alcohol. His drinking had been noticeable since the late 1960s and there had been no let up. He had, since the time of Kingsley Hall, and after leaving Villa 21, become more reclusive and I suspect that he found more spiritual or, at least, less threatening comfort in his tiny flat just off the Eiffel Tower. Admitted to hospital in order to dry out, he returned home after a month before succumbing to a cardio-vascular accident: he was 55.

Note

1. From *Zone of the Interior* by Clancy Sigal (1976). New York: Thomas Y. Crowell. Reproduced with permission from Clancy Sigal.

References

Barham, P. (1997) *Closing the Asylum*. London: Penguin.

Campling, P. and Haigh, R. (1999) *Therapeutic Communities, Past, Present and Future*. London: Jessica Kingsley Publishers.

Clarke, L. (1996) 'Participant observation in a secure unit: care, conflict and control.' *Nursing Times Research 1*, 6, 431–440.

Clay, J. (1996) *R.D. Laing: A Divided Self*. London: Hodder and Stoughton.

Coleman, R. (1999) *Recovery an Alien Concept?* Gloucester: Handsell.

Cooper, D. (1967) *Psychiatry and Anti-psychiatry*. London: Tavistock Publications.

Cooper, D. (1968) *The Dialectics of Liberation*. Harmondsworth: Penguin Books.

Cooper, D. (1971) *The Death of the Family*. London: Allen Lane, The Penguin Press.

Cooper, D. (1976) *The Grammar of Living*. Harmondsworth: Pelican Books.

Farmer, M. (1979) *The Family*. London: Longman.

Foucault, M. (1971) *Madness and Civilisation: A History of Insanity in the Age of Reason*. London: Tavistock Publications.

Kennard, D. (1983) *An Introduction to Therapeutic Communities*. London: Routledge and Kegan Paul.

Lacey, R. (1983) 'David Cooper: Interview by Ron Lacey.' *Openmind 3*, 8–9.

Laing, A. (1994) *R.D. Laing: A Biography*. London: Peter Owen Publishers.

Laing, A. (1997) *R.D. Laing: A Life*. London: Harper Collins.

Martin, D. (1970) 'R.D. Laing.' In M. Cranston (ed) *The New Left*. London: The Bodley Head.

Masters, B. (1985) *The Swinging Sixties*. London: Constable.

Menzies, I. (1960) *Social Systems as a Defence Against Anxiety*. London: Tavistock Publications.

Morgan, D.H.J. (1975) *Social Theory and the Family*. London: Routledge and Kegan Paul Ltd.

O'Callaghan Hernton, (formerly Garvey) M. (2003) Personal communication.

Pullen, G. (1999) 'Schizophrenia: hospital communities for the severely disturbed.' In P. Campling and R. Haigh (eds) *Therapeutic Communities: Past, Present and Future*. London: Jessica Kingsley Publishers.

Shanley, E. (1999) Personal communication.

Shoenberg, E. (1980) 'Therapeutic communities: the ideal, the real and the possible.' In E. Jansen (ed) *The Therapeutic Community*. London: Croom Helm.

Sigal, C. (1976) *Zone of the Interior*. New York: Thomas Y. Crowell.

Skolnick, A. (1973) *The Intimate Environment*. Boston: Little, Brown and Co.

Towell, D. (1975) *Understanding Psychiatric Nursing*. London: Royal College of Nursing.

Wilson, A. (1985) *Family*. London: Tavistock.

Wilson, C. (1956) *The Outsider*. London: Gollancz.

CHAPTER 8

Concluding Therapeutic Communities

> What is this environment or social system that nourishes and fosters growth and creativity? It would seem that it is an open social system operating at a high level of development and growth. We do much talking about the traits of a creative individual. I am suggesting that these traits…are equally applicable to a creative open social environment.
>
> Maxwell Jones (1982)

Introduction

In his Maxwell Jones Memorial Lecture, Professor of Community Psychiatry Tom Burns recalls that Jones:

> wanted to change and manipulate important relationships in order to make their nature clearer, not to trivialise or obliterate them. The very last thing he would have wanted was for them to have been denied because they were uncomfortable. (Burns 2000, p.173)

There are paradoxes here, some of which we've already touched on. If one ventures close to uncomfortable relationships then one necessarily embraces conflict. Jones advocated this for others: he opted to do it himself in some of the most stratified and rigid micro-social systems on earth, namely mental hospitals. The paradox was that in order to risk discomfort from the blurring of roles – which resulted from his abolition of boundaries and hierarchies – he had to utilise the inherent powers of his doctor role, traditionally the least blurred role of all. Unsurprisingly, those most uncomfortable with, because unclear about, their roles – the nurses – had the most difficulty coping with change. In a study of the implementation of therapeutic community principles within a forensic system (Clarke 1999) many of the nurses were found to be experiencing ethical and emotional difficulties. Whilst some of them seemed firmly committed to the fundamentals of the approach – as defined by the Rapoport (1960) version of communalism, reality confrontation, permissiveness and democratisation – another group were vehemently opposed, preferring the security aspects of forensic practice and the maintenance of distinct lines of engagement – emotional, professional – between themselves and their patients.

What was interesting in this study was that the pro-therapeutic community group also linked in to ideas of psychotherapy and an approach that was broadly psycho-social and rehabilitative. It was interesting because although this group was merely paying lip service to what they imagined a therapeutic community to be, this still had the effect of kindling positive working practices. To return to Professor Burns:

> I have talked at length about the issues of role blurring and hierarchy within teams, because I think that they are important. Simply to accept however, the outward manifestations of the therapeutic community movement (e.g. all on first name terms, sitting in groups, a pleasant bohemian style of operating) would be to betray the origins and purposes of this movement. (Burns 2000, p.73)

We shall turn to origins and purposes in a moment. In the forensic study (Clarke 1999) it was precisely the whiff of bohemianism which antagonised the security conscious nurses; their irked reactions – confided in interviews – to the blurring of nurse/patient roles and their wilder apprehensions of nurse/patient intimacy were made plain. Stranger than this, however, was that the pro-therapeutic community group had not read Rapoport's (1960) book, taking the reality of 'the four principles' at face value. They seemed oblivious that Rapoport had applied these terms to the behaviours of a Henderson team not all of whom agreed with them. That said, the four principles have not lost their charm, possessing still a capacity to enthuse and motivate therapeutic work: Hirons (2002), for one, says that they infuse the philosophy of the Benchley Unit, a day therapeutic community which opened in 1999, and the Cedars Community, Rampton Hospital, which opened in 2002 (Bennion 2002). Even when misunderstood, the diversity of values contained within these principles invariably leads towards civilised working practices.

Ups and downs

Since their heyday in the Fifties, Sixties and Seventies, therapeutic communities have had their ups and downs. Bowen and Staedler (2002) chronicle the post-Sixties trials and tribulations of a particular community, itemising its threatened closure but also its changing functions as an outcome of government fiscal policy. Styling itself as a national catchment unit, this community was able to ride the waves of Thatcherism: post Thatcher, however, different pressures emerged: 'Labour government changes to funding, away from extra contractual referrals, meant the ward lost its fiscal *raison d'etre* overnight' (Bowen and Staedler 2002, p.34).

Local NHS Trusts lost their enthusiasm for communities whose catchment areas extended beyond the responsibilities of a given Trust. From here on, each Trust would look to its own. Even (ostensibly) minor events rang the changes of accountability for many communities. Rayner (1989, p.xxi) recalls an incident during the 1980s at the Cassel Hospital where staff congregated each morning for free coffee and an informal chat. NHS managers, cottoning on to this, insisted that staff pay for the coffee. The upshot was that people stopped attending and, says Rayner, an important arena for doing business was lost. There is something to understand here no doubt: psychologically minded people are sometimes aghast at the 'unthinking' pragmatism of health managers and their dedication to good housekeeping. On the other hand, if the meeting was *that* precious, why did the cost of a coffee lead to its demise? Rayner notes that the incident led to 'raised tempers' which may have been justified given the unit's history. Others, seeing things in a broader political context, might view the raised tempers as an expression of arrogance borne of a unit that had had its own way for far too long. The incident becomes a metaphor for a health service moving towards stricter accountability and clearer evidence of best practice.

Accountability would prove a serious stumbling block for some. Bowen and Staedler, canvassing various groups of therapeutic community staff, discovered a siege mentality not unlike that which characterised some communities in the past:

> The powerful world outside the community is viewed at best as an indifferent bystander to our deviant practices…at worst it is actively hostile, for example forcing us to understand ourselves through a discourse alien to us. (Bowen and Staedler 2002, p.39)

Yet why should therapeutic community staff expect the 'wider community' to speak their language or share their perspectives? Whatever became of Maxwell Jones's and T.P. Rees's advice to educate the wider world, to be cognisant of the needs of immediate localities? Coming full circle, communities would now have to look to the needs (and ambitions) of NHS Trusts of which many of them were now subjects.

Therapeutic community closures

Commenting on the rush of closures during the 1990s, Barnes-Gutteridge notes that whilst the consensus view is that these resulted from cuts in public spending this is to confuse causes with effects:

> An important contributory cause of the crisis was the informed public's hostility to and scepticism about psychoanalysis, psychodynamic approaches to therapy and, by association, therapeutic communities. (Barnes-Gutteridge 2002, p.61)

Here, Barnes-Gutteridge is not referring to the public at large but to social workers, psychiatrists, psychologists and policy makers and he alleges that many communities had failed to persuade this 'public', during the 1980s and 1990s, that they had viable therapies for patients with severe mental disabilities. This failure stands in stark contrast to a re-invigorated biological psychiatry which, for 40 years, had been biding its time as 'the social experiments' had their turn.

The US Congress declared the 1990s the 'Decade of the Brain', in effect the tail end of a millennium in which brain sciences would unravel the latent secrets of mental disease and end four decades of fruitless dialectics on the meaning of madness. Charles Golden and Jana Sawicki (1985) were typical of those seeking to invest the 1990s with prophetic powers. Convinced that 'neurological approaches present effective methods of investigating psychopathological disorders', they asserted that 'such approaches will be among the major contributions of the last years of this century'. In his Maxwell Jones Lecture, Tom Burns touched on this: 'We are now being exhorted to re-badge mental illnesses as brain illnesses. The research thrust was directed towards biochemical, pharmacological and imaging studies of the brain' (Burns 2000, p.165).

The term 'evidence-based practice' arrived with a vengeance and discussions – bordering on the quarrelsome – on the relative merits/demerits of qualitative versus quantitative research became common. Psychiatric practitioners faced demands to verify their work and show which interventions for which patients were effective. This proved difficult for therapeutic community practitioners particularly those with leanings towards psychoanalysis, notoriously resistant to 'outside' scrutiny. Indeed, the present writer (Clarke 1993) had once compared training in psychoanalysis to that of a noviciate in monastic religion.

For those working within the Maxwell Jones tradition, things were less fraught. In 1960, Jones had famously invited Robert Rapoport to study the Henderson even if (as it turned out) its findings might not be favourable. Since then, studies of therapeutic communities have multiplied although mostly of the qualitative or ethnographic type. By the 1990s, psychiatry, having re-entered its 'biological phase', began to champion scientific (and especially randomised control trial) studies. To some extent, qualitative designs, now fairly typical of therapeutic community research, were looked on suspiciously. I have discussed the ramifications of this elsewhere (Clarke and Flanagan 2003) and argued for the appropriateness of qualitative designs for investigating social settings, making the point that quantitative research often skews questions away from areas of experiential and interpersonal importance. As we move on from the 1990s, there is now some recognition that research strategies should avoid marginalising human perspectives and experiences.

Learning from experience

The problem is that therapeutic communities have shown only a limited capacity to learn from experience, partly due to an absence of coherent theoretical perspectives. Writing about units for 'troubled children and young people', Barnes-Gutteridge (2002) suggests using psychodynamics so as to clarify the relationship of treatments to effectiveness. In respect of evidence of effectiveness, he advocates comparative studies based on the biographies of children (and their progress) both within and between communities. The problem is that considerable differences exist between children's units so that comparing variables becomes difficult: needless to say, few empirical studies exist into how effective such units might be. Perhaps a more fundamental question, in terms of the place of therapeutic communities within psychiatry generally, is the question of their clientele. Barnes-Gutteridge (2002) provides 'essential indictors' which, he argues, can show that effective therapy has been implemented. These are: the ability of a client to hold down a job, the ability to make authentic relationships, the ability to stay out of prison and the ability to stay out of psychiatric hospital. The first three of these suggest problems that are essentially social and/or deviant in nature: it is unclear that these children are psychiatrically ill. In the case of maladjusted children few would deny the importance of health and social service provision as well as the importance of avoiding narrow psychiatric frameworks. With adults, matters are different and a concept of 'serious and enduring' has been introduced to determine the provision of services which, the NHS now accepts, are finite. We have somehow acquired a moral imperative to regard *some* mental 'conditions' as more serious than others. Within current financial restrictions it becomes a priority to keep all but the most seriously ill out of psychiatric units: further, if we accept that some people *are* mentally ill, then it becomes difficult to see them as having retained a full range of cognitive abilities. Where patients lose their autonomy (in the Kantian sense) then the kinds of criteria listed by Barnes-Gutteridge become redundant since, in the context of serious mental illness, the capacity for rational thought is lost. This mounting concern about 'serious and enduring' illness drives the search for tighter forms of research and evidence: the political context, in particular, favours high-lighting psychotic patients especially in respect of dangerousness and perceived public anxiety about this. Public monies, therefore, will follow studies which focus on more discrete medical and/or psychological illnesses, treatments and their outcomes.

Borderline personality states

To some extent, therapeutic communities have steered clear of this discussion because of their commitment to serving people with personality disorders, the category of clients for whom they have claimed some therapeutic success. Within general psychiatry there persists an age-old antipathy towards these clients (Clarke 1999; May and Kelly 1982) who are usually seen as wilful and acting from a psychological position of control (even deviousness), and unlike psychotics who are seen as out of control and therefore not responsible. It is a simplistic view and fraught with philosophical problems about what counts as 'insight' and 'out of control', but it has a long lineage.

And, in any event, throughout history, in most societies, beliefs have existed that some people suffer madness and become in need of special provision. Many practitioners see these patients as comprising 'the coal face' of psychiatry, with other categories relegated to second fiddle. At the same time, psychiatry feels morally obligated to 'manage' difficult individuals who are of concern to society. Apparently free from illness, these personality disor-dered people – disruptive, cynical, manipulative, narcissistic – may refuse therapy perhaps in an attempt to invalidate the helping role. If psychotic patients display ingratitude they are perceived to do so through lack of insight whereas the non-compliance of the sociopath is seen as deliberate and possibly malevolent.

Major contribution

It was the major contribution of therapeutic communities to begin to think around these problems *psychologically*, to develop understandings of antipa-thies and try to resolve them. It is not a complete surprise that modern forensic psychiatry, charged with containing anti-social patients, has sought to mimic therapeutic community practice, although, as noted, not without controversy. Part of this controversy surrounds the effectiveness (and appropriateness) of psychotherapy for people who spurn civilised discourse and whose needs must be weighted against society's right to protection. It is a situation that is wide open to investigation: can therapeutic community principles be utilised with legally detained (incarcerated) patients who are resistive to change? More importantly, what would indicate a 'successful utilisation'? One approach would be to match group therapy with some patients against no therapy for a control group and independently assess outcomes across a range of externally validated criteria. Whilst such approaches are not to everyone's taste, they are becoming standard, especially where public funding is involved. However, before examining this, we need to delve into the possible connections between causes, therapies and outcomes.

Behaviourism and psychoanalysis

There may be little connection between the causal factors of someone's problems and proposed solutions to them: David Malan observed:

> In the case of obsessional symptoms and particularly obsessional rituals it is often the disappearance of symptoms that is not fulfilled – in other words everything becomes intelligible and the patient becomes conscious of the conflict, but therapeutic results do not ensue. It is apparently true, for instance, that no authenticated case of an obsessional handwasher being cured by psychoanalytic treatment has ever come to light. Correspondingly, as far as learning theory and behaviour therapy are concerned, the symptoms improve but a clear formulation of what the symptoms represent does not emerge. (Malan 1979, p.107)

Malan's call for an integrated approach to theory and outcome is echoed by contemporary therapeutic community writers: in a passage that echoes Malan's concerns, Barnes-Gutteridge states:

> Outcome studies by themselves, though, are insufficient. At best they might uncover the paradigm patterns of life experience that are *associated* with troubled behaviour; they cannot provide an understanding of why particular patterns of life experience might *cause* the troubled behaviour. (Barnes-Gutteridge 2002, p.72)

What is required, in addition to outcome studies, is a theoretical perspective which indicates why some clients are predisposed to act as they do: such a perspective would identify experiences that underlie clients' troubles and identify the specifics of such troubled behaviour for which a method of therapy might be effective. Such concerns about objectives and clinical audit have gradually come to preoccupy therapeutic community practitioners. For example, Gatiss and Pooley (2001) have outlined a model which stresses, from the psychodynamic tradition, an emphasis on attachment and the possibilities for unconscious communication between client and therapist. Although this stops short of mapping and measuring discrete interventions, defining the *nature* of interventions is a step in the right direction.

User movements

Psychiatric user movements may be the ultimate vindication of the democratic principles which fuelled therapeutic community practice. Although heterogeneous by nature, user groups have generally been sceptical about conventional psychiatry, preferring approaches which emphasise relationships and rejecting models based on professional power.

All therapeutic communities collapsed staff and patient levels into each other – flattened their hierarchies – and some see in this the start of the user movement as we now know it: but this is debatable. User groups are comprised mainly of psychotic patients whereas therapeutic communities have, on the whole, not catered for such patients. One which did, Street Ward at Fulbourn Hospital (1975–1979), is:

> probably still the most sustained and intensive British attempt that has been made to run an orthodox acute admission ward as a therapeutic community; most of its patients were in an acute phase of a psychotic illness. (Pullen 1999, p.142)

But Street Ward only counts as a therapeutic community within a very broad definition of what a community is. A good number of its patients, for instance, were treated against their will and such coercion seems, quite simply, to contradict therapeutic community practice which clearly implies that participants assent to treatment. Stretching definitions to include compulsion fatally contaminates the essence of what communities have traditionally represented. Even Pullen (1999) acknowledges that communities are a difficult concept on this point. They also become an improbable proposition if participants are actively psychotic for long periods. When they are, the psychotic therapeutic community will undergo genuine difficulty in disallowing the (traditional) divisions which determine staff and client relationships.

According to Tucker (2001), the under-representation of psychotic patients in therapeutic communities is due to the Phenothiazine drugs which conceptually 'explained' psychosis as well as providing for its effective treatment. This makes some sense, but it evades the issue that many psychotic people might not be *able* to function within a therapeutic community. Could someone with schizophrenia cope with continuous group sessions, or an ambience in which reality confrontation and permissiveness might exacerbate an already insufficient ego strength? Perhaps, perhaps not. The problem with thinking not, is that it triggers therapeutic pessimism and leads, ultimately, to the kinds of ritual responses that constitute institutionalism. It was, gratifyingly, therapeutic community practice which put paid to such reductive, 'inborn and irredeemable', beliefs. But, as noted in Chapter 2, in the mental hospitals its principles were applied in a watered-down fashion consistent with maintaining the custodial modalities to which these hospitals subscribed but also, one imagines, with an awareness that the patient population was simply unsuitable. All in all, the atypicality of psychosis in therapeutic community history hardly accounts for its current ascendancy within user movements, and tracing the origins of such movements back into the therapeutic community seems an odd thing to do.

Tucker makes connections between communities, user groups and the growing emphasis on psychological treatments for psychoses. She sees cognitive treatments as a shift in emphasis from objectivity to subjectivity and that this:

> has led to an emphasis on talking treatments for psychosis where clients are given the full opportunity to speak about their experiences and thoughts and this in itself is seen to be of therapeutic value. (Tucker 2001, p.236)

She denotes the user movement as the end result of client participation within therapeutic communities – particularly the communities associated with R.D. Laing and David Cooper – and sees them as forerunners of 'current trends for the psychological and social treatment of psychosis' (Tucker 2001, p.238). Such connections, in my view, are tenuous. Whilst the British Psychological Society (2000) is advocating such approaches this is due to the pre-eminence of cognitive-behaviourism within contemporary clinical psychology as well as aspirations towards greater professional independence.

Cognitive-behaviourism, although it evolved outside clinical psychiatry, nevertheless resembles it by emphasising the central role of the therapist. True, the *aim* of cognitive therapy resembles the therapeutic community desire to give clients some control over their lives; however, the *methods* used for this are different. Further, whilst some cognitive behaviourists assert that their methods apply to most disorders, including psychosis, equally there are many who disagree.

Yet, whilst this analysis may seem plausible, closer inspection reveals uncertainties. Firstly, as Tucker acknowledges, user *movements* is probably more accurate than user movement; diversity is the key. More importantly, some service users resent being defined by professionals in any shape or form. For example, Peter Campbell agrees that anti-psychiatry did influence the emergence of user groups in the 1980s but says that this inheritance was 'emotional and spiritual rather than programmatic and pragmatic' (Campbell 1996, p.221).

In fact, the confrontational tendency of some user groups (over the last 20 years) has been more heavily influenced by foreign than home-grown activists particularly from the USA and the Netherlands. Campbell also asserts that whatever the successes of service users in forcing a consideration of them as partners in health care, mentally ill people remain at risk from prejudice and discrimination. Moreover, given that concepts of (and concerns about) dangerousness have *increased*, the mentally unwell are more – not less – likely to suffer discrimination. Changing this means challenging large numbers of people with directly contrary ideas. A criticism of therapeutic communities is that they have tended to inhabit self-made worlds cut off from the everyday concerns of general psychiatric practice. This was the basis of T.P. Rees's accusation about the Tavistock burying its head in psychoanalytic sand whilst psychotic patients got a raw deal in the hospitals. Equally, whilst Cooper and Laing produced complex blends of Phenomenology, Marxism and an uneasy Libertarianism this also had little to do with the problems confronting most (state funded) patients at the time.

Laing and Cooper

Despite appearances to the contrary, Laing and Cooper were strange bedfellows: Laing never shared Cooper's socialist 'vision' (socialist chic is more apt), not that either of them demonstrated much commitment to institutional or other social change. In Cooper's case, Geoffrey Pullen states that at Villa 21, when the going got rough, Cooper simply quit. Similarly, Laing's work with schizophrenic 'families' quickly palled and when it did he simply dropped it. What united Cooper and Laing, however, was the value they placed on the experiences of psychotic people. This idea is currently regaining psychiatric favour and various groups are claiming it as their province. However, Laing and Cooper approached this question in a different way to others. Most professionals insist that psychotic experiences are problematic – a psychological rather than physiological problem, perhaps, but a problem nonetheless. Agreed, many service users might concur with this; but equally, some would object to being conceptualised as ill at all. This is important because it was Laing's idea – that the psychotic experience be respected not made problematic – that led to his estrangement from psychiatry. So long as the psychotic was conceived as an object – even when, as in *The Divided Self*, the objectification was 'radical' – then psychiatry could safely exhibit itself as an abstract system, the patient defined within established physiological, psychological, sociological or even spiritual dimensions. Laing and Cooper strayed outside these domains and it was that which anathematised them.

Freedom from treatment?

In the typical (non-psychotic) units it becomes possible to rope *everybody* into the same psychological framework: for example, discussing inherent paradoxes within therapeutic communities Jane Knowles observes, 'Where all is apparently democratic, where patients are empowered, where staff are tools of and for the group, none the less the emotional exchanges feed staff psychopathology' (Knowles 2001, p.274).

Of such stuff are psychoanalytic dreams made: many communities thrive on such self-absorption as a prelude to working through and shriving off neuroses, rages and depressions. There is an assumption that no essential psychopathology separates staff and patient groups. But what of psychosis? That, as W.C. Fields would say, 'is an equine of a different hue', and much more difficult to deal with, especially in terms of user advocacy and self-determination. The problem is at its most acute when looking at people who are actually receiving treatment. How much leeway do users have for self-advocacy at this point? Or is self-advocacy a post-care, post-treatment phenomenon? The difficulty is that psychosis increases demands on professional input: this is also true in severe learning disabilities where there is a necessary reliance on interpreters and go-betweens. The issue is central because of allegations that since user groups are not actively ill, then their involvement in health care provision is a charade. This is an allegation that is both true and stupid. True because when distressed by illness, it is unlikely that *anyone* would be able to advocate for themselves: stupid, because what is so surprising about someone who is ill being incapacitated? Surely that holds true for anyone. Neither does it affect the capacity to resume one's critique when recovery takes place. And, of course, in the meantime, the user may have set up a protocol designed to govern their progress *when* ill – a bit like a pre-nuptial agreement. That said, if on becoming mentally unwell, a service user participated in, for example, committee meetings, then that could be problematic if his or her behaviour was affected by hearing voices. There is no answer to this, although the overriding principle has to be that it is for users to demand non-token service involvement; it is not in the gift of professionals but it is this which is most problematic.

Where we are now

In Hopton's review, the factors which most frequently count as appropriate therapeutic community practice are 'a culture of inquiry, communalism, democracy, permissiveness, reality confrontation' (Hopton 2000, p.9). So: no change there; the essential, egalitarian, characteristics of therapeutic communities remain the same, at least as reflected in the literature. This egalitarianism may partly account for the decline of communities during the autocratic 1980s and 1990s although, in the light of emergent user movements, the decline is surprising. However, user involvement probably reflects increasing pressures from patients/consumers and their organisations generally – for example in obstetrics and gynaecology. Add to this general perceptions of institutional and community psychiatric failure and you have all the grounds needed for vibrant user movements.

In respect of their egalitarianism, conventional psychiatry had never been comfortable with therapeutic communities even if content (or clever) enough to assimilate some of their more workable aspects. Knowles notes how communities have 'had a rocky time, many of them falling along the wayside, victim to the very real hostility and envy of so many critical elder sisters in psychiatry' (Knowles 2001, p.275).

Strange how 'outside' criticism is often seen as hostile and never as the pragmatic concern of those who may have to 'foot the bill'. From the 1980s onwards, growing awareness of the need for evidence-based practice resulted in more controlled descriptions of both the nature of communities and their effectiveness. The two issues are related in so far as changes in patients (outcomes) require therapists to declare what has brought change about (nature).

To that end, some practitioners began to inquire after good practice: Kennard and Lees produced a checklist of features:

> that can be used to accredit a therapeutic community, which are concrete enough to be objectively assessed as present to a greater or lesser degree, but at the same time reflect the daily living learning experience of a therapeutic community in a way that practitioners will recognise as a true picture of what they do or try to do. (Kennard and Lees 2001, p.143–144)

The checklist represents an advance because it expresses what counts as 'good' community practice. However, its broad array of interventions incurs the age-old charge that therapeutic communities lack specificity about why they are curative or even effective. As the 1990s proceeded, what was now needed were measures of effectiveness and patient outcome studies. This was not to everyone's liking but it was difficult to resist where politically inspired indices such as hospital performance lists and other indicators of 'excellence' had become de rigueur. What would grate, however, was the *nature* of the evidence sought by organisations such as NICE (National Institute for Clinical Excellence) which appeared to favour quantitative research. Such evidence is not the easiest to retrieve from investigations into social systems of care. An indication of troubles to come was the recent resignation of service user Louise Pembroke (James 2003) from a NICE committee charged with examining self-harm. Pembroke accused the committee of favouring medically oriented data whilst rejecting the substantial qualitative material available from service users.

Of course, some therapeutic community theorists might not *want* to do comparative studies or produce effectiveness statistics for their work: there exists, amongst some, a tendency to mimic the late Don Bannister who damned the concept of effectiveness altogether. In Bannister's view (1998 reprint), demands for effectiveness constitute a moral imperative which should be challenged. Attending to individuals (arguably the heart of psychotherapy) is equally a moral act since it cherishes the experience of the client's standpoint. Bannister was surely right that only through valuing the personal can we eradicate malign forms of institutional care. He went on to say:

> If our experience of psychological therapy makes sense to us, that is to say we can see reasons why we have been of no help to this person or some help to that person and we find that we can develop and elaborate our understanding through our work, we are likely to continue to work this way *whatever the literature may say*. (Bannister 1998, p.219)

Commenting on Bannister's paper, Miller Mair (1998, p.220) said: 'this little piece should be required reading for people in all professions engaging in therapeutic conversation. I especially like the last paragraph':

> My contention is that we should work as psychologists not as psychic paramedics. Our language, research methods and theory should be drawn from psychology and not from an imprisoning imitation of medical treatment studies. (Bannister 1998, p.220)

Classically, this is the departure point for alternative constructs of therapy, that medicalisation inhibits ordinary language and relationships whereas social and analytic concepts generate freer, more discursive, spaces from within which change can occur.

A place apart

Discussing the meaning of 'place' Anne Salway says that 'the therapeutic community is a sacred territory, a place set apart' (Salway 2001, p.176). Referring to a Kingsley Hall resident who took to his bed for two years, Salway turns to a quote from Robin Cooper about how this resident could have been helped: 'Not at any rate by "helping" having to be seen to be engaged in some sort of propriety activity such that the possibilities of attentive non intervention are unquestionably pre-empted' (Cooper 1989, p.53). By doing nothing, life, as it passes, is permitted the space by which to recapture the man's attention which, in this case, it apparently did. Says Cooper: 'Beyond what is going on, there is nothing' (Cooper 1989, p.55).

As we shall see, passivity is winning conscripts again. Barker and Stevenson (2002), for example, outline a Tidal Model where clients' experiences must take their course unimpeded, becoming the foundation for growth and well-being. These processes are asserted to be self-evident and resolutely not open to empirical, positivist, inquiry.

Critics have quickly identified a messianic unwillingness to compare their model with other interventions. For example, Gamble and Wellman state that the only way to evaluate whether such approaches:

> make a real difference to patient outcomes…would be in a carefully planned and fairly large-scale clinical trial. Such a trial would specify the outcomes of interest in advance, agree how these outcomes would be measured and by whom and would have a planned sample size, calculated to ensure that adequate statistical power would be achieved. (Gamble and Wellman 2002, p.742)

Looked at in comparison, Salway's 'position' (above) suggests that more than minor differences are involved, that there are two separate worlds here: the one philosophical, experiential, poetic, even spiritual; the other desiring to account for itself in scientific, factual terms. The problem is that factual approaches, despite claims to the contrary, are difficult to apply in social settings and Hotopf (2002) has ably demonstrated how quantitative designs can prove self-defeating when seeking to explain human action. Aficionados of randomised controlled trials have over-stated their applicability within social systems and, in their desire for scientific respectability, have even exaggerated their utility so as to generate unconfounded conclusions. That said, claims to therapeutic effectiveness need to make use of outcome measures to *some* extent. The Bannister position is hardly sufficient where psychotic people are struggling with problems in their lives and with therapists laying claim to helping them. Barker and Stevenson accuse Gamble and Wellman of looking for:

> a method that can be shown to be economically, statistically or politically 'better' than some other. [We] have no such interest in delimiting, defining and prescribing any such method. (Barker and Stevenson 2002, p.744)

Instead, communication is asserted as the essence of all psychological therapies and which 'can never be tested in a neo positivistic way' (p.744). If this is true, then it appears we have an impasse.

Resolution

The conundrum is, what counts as therapy and what is its relationship to philosophy? In the formative years of psychotherapy, at the end of the 19th century, both existentialist (Binswanger 1963; Boss 1963) and psychoanalytic (Freud 1971) practitioners were concerned about the philosophical/scientific implications of their positions and, for some of them, this remained the case. Tavistock psychotherapy, for example, initially invited sneers from some who preferred to engage their principles in a more diffuse, more philosophical way. In fact, there is no necessary link between philosophy and therapy (Farrell 1963) at all. This can be seen in David Malan's (1979) contention that no cases of obsessive compulsive disorder had ever been successfully treated with psychoanalysis. This might prove fatal to psychoanalysis but only if you believe in analysis as a psychotherapy. Contrariwise, we know that cognitive-behaviour therapy *is* effective in treating obsessive compulsive disorders; its success rates are excellent. But does cognitive-behaviourism successfully withstand scrutiny as a philosophy of human behaviour or morals? Malan didn't think so and neither do I. However, this doesn't impinge on it being an effective therapy.

Which is not to say that effectiveness is without its problems. Ends do not justify means and, in psychiatry, there is always a danger in over valuing what works at the expense of ethics. Yet, however philosophically sophisticated a psychiatric model might be, outcome studies remain important, else why apply these 'philosophies' in psychiatric settings? However philosophically enlightened one's approach, applying it within a psychiatric context is to invite questions about effectiveness. For communities whose purpose is exploration or enlightenment – such as monasteries – performance indices are not required; but where there is an intention to modify behaviour, then some effectiveness measure is required.

Randomisation versus socialisation

When setting up Villa 21, David Cooper was acutely aware of the dichotomy between experimental methods and methods which mapped subjects' experiences. He favoured the latter but noted how:

> Immediate objections are raised when an investigation of this sort is proposed: where are your controls? How are you going to quantify any of your material? How can you claim any generality for your statements on the basis of only a small number of cases? (Cooper 1970, p.17)

He argued that 'proof' is an *a priori* impossibility when researching social encounters because of the continuity between subjects even when occupying the roles of observed and observer. Reeking of 1960s sociologese, Cooper expressed the difficulty thus:

> I totalise you but you, in your reciprocal totalisation of me, include my totalisation of you, so that my totalisation of you involves a totalisation of your totalisation of me, and so on. (Cooper 1970, pp.20–21)

Whilst potentially risible, this does confront the dilemma of achieving objectivity in respect of subjects; how does one distance oneself so as to report findings unambiguously? Even in the radical Sixties, he dutifully attaches a 'results' section in his description of Villa 21 (Cooper 1970, pp.124–137). He did this, he says, because 'there are at least strategic reasons for looking at the work in terms of one of the less objectionable psychiatric criteria of improvement' (Cooper 1970, p.124). Disdaining quantitative analysis, he still presents statistical material to show how his re-admission rates compare well to those of conventionally treated patients. His problem – and that of modern therapeutic communities – is that he couldn't precisely state what the treatment was.

A comprehensive review

In 1999 Lees, Manning and Rawlings stated:

> There is meta-analytic and clinical evidence that therapeutic communities produce changes in people's mental health and functioning, but this needs to be further complemented by good quality qualitative and quantitative research studies. (Lees *et al.* 1999, p.8)

They acknowledge that research on effectiveness has been poor and that more rigorous studies are now needed. In their report, they set out to 'Evaluate the extent, nature, validity and reliability of existing research' (Lees *et al.* 1999, p.14). A tall order. The study is complicated by including studies reported world-wide and across different types of community. Examining 'treatment outcome studies', they found only one randomised control trial. In addition, they found that most single case studies did not have control or comparison groups. In terms of post-treatment outcome studies, they found three random-ised control trials but these were over 30 years old. They also discovered that more recent studies (Chiesa 1997; Piper *et al.* 1996) of this type exhibited major methodological flaws. This is important because experimental studies, especially randomised controlled trials, are seen by some as 'the gold standard' whereas qualitative studies – for instance analyses of individual units or their comparison with other units – are seen as less rigorous. According to Lees *et al.*, 'There is no intrinsic reason why randomised control trials should not be mounted further for therapeutic communities. However [they] are difficult to run for therapeutic Communities' (Lees *et al.* 1999, p.99), and this is what they found – experimental studies where outcome measures were crudely idiosyncratic to the particular institutions involved. Attrition rates tended to be high as were problems in the random allocation of subjects. Above all, variations in what are nowadays *called* therapeutic communities made it very difficult to ensure treatment integrity when comparing outcomes.

Proving effectiveness

The problem for therapists today is how to satisfy the NHS that their work is clinically effective. This is confounded by what government agencies will accept as evidence. The National Service Framework (1999) gives a low priority to qualitative evidence: it associates evidence-based practice with quantitative studies, qualitative work being seen as somehow second rate and anecdotal. But such narrow empiricism surely limits the range and depth of investigations where people's experiences are seen as relevant. What counts as evidence rests on what one wishes to ask and the contexts in which it is asked. From time immemorial, all medical specialities have relied upon symptoms (what patients report) as much as on signs (biological manifestations) when di-agnosing illness. This dual concern underscores conceptual differences between illness and disease. Whilst the latter is described as pathology, the former rests as much on clients' experiences and how they interpret them. Because human behaviour is important, discursive methods may be the only means of gathering data which can be meaningfully related to outcomes. Discussing the importance of everyday terms, Mary Midgley states:

> Words such as *care, heart, spirit, sense,* [her italics] are tools designed for particular kinds of work in the give-and-take of social life... They are not a cheap substitute, an inadequate folk psychology, due to be replaced by the proper terms of the learned. (Midgley 2001, p.11)

Putting this into a context of therapy, Don Bannister (1998 reprint) says, 'if you were asked how effective is conversation you would surely begin by questioning the question. As it stands it is nonsense' (Bannister 1998, p.218). For Bannister, the very notion of effectiveness *is* a nonsense:

> Are you really prepared to contend that your relationships, your love affairs, your enmities, your long standing dialogue with your uncle Albert – whether the effect be good, bad or chaotic – have been, in some strange sense, ineffective? (Bannister 1998, p.219)

He has a point. However, reflect for a moment: if one concedes that psychotherapy has the same standing as family relationships, then no more than what ordinarily prevails, ethically, between relatives is required. But is there not an ethical shift when conducting therapy with strangers, a shift requiring the pronouncement of therapeutic aims or expectations? Doesn't the professional role involve *some* assumptions about alleviating psychological distress as well as *some* commitment to showing that this in fact happens?

So what is to be changed or altered by therapy? To my mind, the issue is not just about the appropriateness of research paradigms. Contemporary fascination with cost-effective, evidence-based, outcomes imply that some problems merit more attention than others. For example, disorders such as schizophrenia or obsessive compulsive disorder are more researchable by experimental designs than mental distress that is entrenched in daily living. This, in turn, stems from beliefs that biological factors determine behaviour and that human discourse contributes little to the research knowledge base. Barham, writing about J.L.T. Birley (1991), President of the Royal College of Psychiatrists says;

> The attempt to disguise mental illness as just like any other sort of illness, is ...the product of a long history of oversimplification and he believes that his colleagues should now abandon the approach of promoting psychiatry as a special form of physical illness. (Barham 1997, p.153)

This means devising suitable methods for describing the progress or otherwise of a range of clients. The problem, as Atkinson *et al.* describe is that:

> Current perspectives on ethnographic research can be characterised in terms of variety. The methodological domain is marked by a clamour of styles and justifications. Not only is there diversity, there are also subversive and transgressive tendencies. (Atkinson *et al.* 2001, p.12)

This 'anything counts' attitude has already hampered qualitative research because it breeds suspicions of theoretical and practical disarray. Defending different types of enquiry falls well short of satisfying criticisms about outcome studies. Therapeutic community researchers are in the un-envious position of finding backing for their studies whilst resisting forms of inquiry that would cheapen their therapeutic traditions.

In the view of Lees *et al.* cross institutional designs point the way forward: these are where:

> A range of therapeutic community treatment interventions in their existing natural state [may be studied and where] different aspects can be unravelled, and can be related to patient change during and after treatment. (Lees *et al.* 1999, p.105)

Massive problems remain however; problems of generalising findings, of accepting the lesser persuasiveness of correlational designs, of being specific about which outcomes are a result of which intervention and why. What is now clear is that outcome studies are at least necessary; it is not enough – actually it has become rather tedious – to read yet more papers on 'the community as sacred space', and so forth, but not because these are uninteresting. Quite the contrary, they define communities as philosophically interesting, but they detract from their reputation as robust centres of therapeutic activity and research. Yes, the therapeutic community impulse is to create spaces where reflective thought can flourish. And within such spaces, the clamour for outcomes and statistical indices can seem degrading. It can also lead to qualitative researchers becoming 'victims' of an unconscious desire to achieve mastery over the research area by appropriating its culture and transforming it into the 'evidence' of what it seeks to communicate (see Rudge 2002, pp.157–158). Perhaps as a reaction to the perceived 'superiority' of experimental designs, 'realities' are invented so as to fit expectations as to what constitutes good research.

At a juncture

Research is driven by profound inquisitiveness about why things are the way they are and therapeutic communities exemplify this. However, they now need to stop 'talking amongst themselves' and acknowledge their wider responsibilities within overall health care. To that end, research needs to focus on effectiveness and begin playing down spiritual, theoretical and/or speculative dimensions. None of this matters if communities are places of retreat, spiritual re-growth or enlightenment: but in so far as they claim therapeutic efficiency, they need to show that this happens.

Rogers and Pilgrim (2003, pp. 67–68) dismiss therapeutic communities for having neglected external social conditions which impinge on mental illness and for allowing themselves to become marginalised into the singular area of personality disorder. In addition, they say, British communities failed to connect with trade unions, as later happened in Italy with the Psychiatrica Democratica movement. This is actually a variant on the old criticism that communities were too elitist, too narcissistic and it is, in this instance, a one-sided view. For example, the implication that social forces *cause* psychosis is doubtful: they may promote or impede its progress. Focusing on personality disorder can be seen as marginalisation; equally can it be viewed as specialisation. Clinical psychiatry itself does this when it concentrates on the psychoses and avoids other forms of mental disability. In other words, a degree of fragmentation – due to internal psychiatric rivalry – has occurred, and bringing in concepts of marginalisation may simply reflect that rivalry. True, the association of therapeutic communities and psychotic patients was hardly fruitful and orthodox psychiatry bears some jealous responsibility for that. But the therapeutic community was never meant to be a panacea.

More recently, the relocation of some communities to 'the community' may bridge some of these gaps. Community Housing and Therapy (2002) are currently supported by 28 Social Service Departments and 10 Health Authorities. It aims to provide individual and group therapies in residential settings for a range of psychiatric disabilities as well as provision for homeless and socially deprived people. Only a minority of their residents are diagnosed with personality disorder; most are diagnosed with schizophrenia. An independent review is needed to show if such ventures correspond to the 'classical' communities established by Maxwell Jones and others. We have seen how the therapeutic community umbrella covers a multitude and that some of its ventures have been morally dubious. But, overall, therapeutic communities have been the 'jewel in the crown' of social psychiatry. They have deployed a psychiatric practice that is humane and which attempts to embrace the experiences of their members. It may be that any psychiatry which places the therapist on an equal – if imperfect – footing with patients will forfeit the scientific credibility that some find precious: but that may be a small price to pay for putting people first.

References

Atkinson, P., Coffey, A. and Delamont, S. (2001) 'A debate about our canon.' *Qualitative Research 1*, 1, 5–21.

Bannister, D. (1998) 'The nonsense of effectiveness.' *Changes 16*, 3, 218–220.

Barham, P. (1997) *Closing the Asylum: The Patient in Modern Society.* London: Penguin Books.

Barker, P. and Stevenson, C. (2002) 'Reply to Gamble and Wellman.' *Journal of Psychiatric and Mental Health Nursing 9*, 741–745.

Barnes-Gutteridge, W. (2002) 'Towards a new generation of therapeutic communities for troubled children and young people.' *Therapeutic Communities 23*, 1, 61–74.

Bennion, L. (2002) 'A TC is born!' *Joint Newsletter of the Association of Therapeutic Communities, the Charterhouse Group and the Planned Environment Therapy Trust 6*, November, 46–47.

Binswanger, L. (1963) *Being-In-The-World.* London: Basic Books.

Birley, J.L.T. (1991) 'Psychiatrists and citizens.' *British Journal of Psychiatry 159*, 1–6.

Boss, M. (1963) *Psychoanalysis and Daseinanalysis.* London: Basic Books.

Bowen, M. and Staedler, G. (2002) 'A living testament to the power of anarchy.' *Therapeutic Communities 23*, 1, 33–44.

British Psychological Society (2000) *Recent Advances in Understanding Mental Illness and Psychotic Experiences.* Leicester: The British Psychological Society.

Burns, T. (2000) 'The legacy of therapeutic community in modern community mental health services.' *Therapeutic Communities 21*, 3, 165–174.

Campell, P. (1996) 'The history of the user movement in the United Kingdom.' In T. Heller, J. Reynolds, R. Gomm, R. Muston and S. Pattison (eds) *Mental Health Matters: A Reader.* London: Macmillan and The Open University.

Chiesa, M. (1997) 'A combined in-patient/out-patient programme for severe personality disorders.' *Therapeutic Communities 18*, 4, 297–309.

Clarke, L. (1993) 'Ordinary miseries: extraordinary remedies.' *British Journal of Psychotherapy 10*, 237–248.

Clarke, L. (1999) *Challenging Ideas in Psychiatric Nursing.* London: Routledge.

Clarke, L. and Flanagan, T. (2003) *Institutional Breakdown.* Salisbury: Academic Publishing Services.

Community Housing and Therapy (2002) *Annual Report.* London: Community Housing and Therapy.

Cooper, D. (1970) *Psychiatry and Anti-psychiatry.* London: Paladin.

Cooper, R. (1989) 'Dwelling and the therapeutic community.' In R. Cooper (ed) *Thresholds Between Philosophy and Psychoanalysis: Papers from the Philadelphia Association.* London: Free Association Books.

Farrell, B.A. (1963) 'Psychoanalysis: the method.' *New Society 39*, 12–13.

Freud, S. (1971) *Introductory Lectures on Psychoanalysis.* London: Allen and Unwin.

Gamble, C. and Wellman, N. (2002) 'Judgement impossible.' *Journal of Psychiatric and Mental Health Nursing 9*, 741–742.

Gatiss, S.J. and Pooley, J. (2001) 'Standards of practice for working with children and young people in a therapeutic community setting.' *Therapeutic Communities 22*, 3, 191–196.

Golden, C.J. and Sawicki, R.F. (1985) 'Neuropsychological bases of psychopathological disorders.' In L.C. Hartlage and C.F. Telzrow (eds) *The Neuropsychology of Individual Differences.* London: Plenum Press.

Hirons, R.M. (2002) 'User involvement in the Benchley Unit – an experiment on democracy.' *Joint Newsletter of the Association of Therapeutic Communities, the Charterhouse Group and the Planned Environment Therapy Trust 6*, November, 20–21.

Hopton, J. (2000) 'Alive and well – but hard to find.' *Openmind 103*, 9.

Hotopf, M. (2002) 'The pragmatic randomised controlled trial.' *Advances in Psychiatric Treatment 8*, 326–333.

James, A. (2003) 'A disparity of esteem.' *Openmind 119*, 13.

Jones, M. (1982) *The Process of Change.* London: Routledge and Keegan Paul.

Kennard, D. and Lees, J. (2001) 'A checklist of standards for democratic therapeutic communities.' *Therapeutic Communities 22*, 2, 143–151.

Knowles, J. (2001) 'TCs – do we need to break free and think afresh?' *Therapeutic Communities 22*, 4, 271–285.

Lees, J., Manning, N. and Rawlings, B. (1999) *Therapeutic Community Effectiveness: CRD Report 17.* York: University of York: NHS Centre For Reviews and Dissemination.

Mair, M. (1998) 'Letter to editor.' *Changes 16*, 3, 220.

Malan, D. (1979) *Individual Psychotherapy and the Science of Psychodynamics.* London: Butterworth.

May, D. and Kelly, M.P. (1982) 'Chancers, pests and poor wee souls: problems of legitimation in psychiatric nursing.' *Sociology of Health and Illness 4*, 279–299.

Midgley, M. (2001) *Science and Poetry.* London: Routledge.

National Service Framework for Mental Health (1999) London: Department of Health.

Piper, W.E., Rosie, J.S., Joyce, A.S. and Azim, H.F.A. (1996) *Time Limited Day Treatment for Personality Disorders: Integration of Research and Practice.* Washington, DC: American Psychological Association.

Pullen, G. (1999) 'Schizophrenia: hospital communities for the severely disturbed.' In P. Campling and R. Haigh (eds) *Therapeutic Communities: Past, Present and Future.* London: Jessica Kingsley Publishers.

Rapoport, R. (1960) *The Community as Doctor.* London: Tavistock Publications.

Rayner, E. (1989) 'Introduction.' In J. Johns and E. Rayner (eds) *The Ailment and Other Psychoanalytic Essays.* London: Free Association Books.

Rogers, A. and Pilgrim, D. (2003) *Mental Health and Inequality.* Basingstoke: Palgrave Macmillan.

Rudge, T. (2002) '(Re)writing ethnography: the unsettling questions for nursing research raised by post-structural approaches in the field.' In A.M. Rafferty and M. Traynor (eds) *Exemplary Research for Nursing and Midwifery.* London: Routledge.

Salway, A. (2001) 'The sacred and the therapeutic community.' *Therapeutic Community 22*, 3, 175–182.

Tucker, S. (2001) 'Psychosis and the therapeutic community: beyond the user movement?' *Therapeutic Communities 22*, 3, 233–247.

Subject Index

Author Index